Exploring Great Basin National Park

Including Mount Moriah Wilderness

Bruce Grubbs

Bright Angel Press

Flagstaff, Arizona

Exploring Great Basin National Park: Including Mount Moriah Wilderness

© 2011-2020 Bruce Grubbs

Updated April 2020

All photos and graphics by the author unless otherwise credited

Bright Angel Press

Flagstaff, Arizona

www.BrightAngelPress.com

ISBN: 978-0-9827130-4-4

While every effort has been made to assure the accuracy of the information in this book, by using this book you take full responsibility for your own safety and recognize that outdoor activities may be hazardous.

Acknowledgments

This book would not have possible without the help of the following people and organizations: First of all, thanks to June Beasley for an excellent copy editing job. Thank you to Betsy Duncan-Clark, Great Basin National Park, and Clare Sorensen, Western National Parks Association, for reviewing the manuscript and providing many helpful suggestions. Their ongoing efforts are making it possible to keep this book up to date. And thanks to Duart Martin for supporting this effort throughout the process.

Contents

Introduction...1

Overview Maps...3

What is the Great Basin?...9

History of the Snake Range..11

Getting to Great Basin National Park............................21

Starting Your Visit...25

Lehman Caves..27

Scenic Drives..29

Lodging and Services..39

Picnicking...41

Camping...43

For Kids and Families...51

Photography..53

Wildflower Viewing...57

Bird Watching..59

Star Gazing...63

Pine Nut Gathering...67

Fishing...69

Horseback Riding...73

Bicycling...75

Hiking..77

Winter Touring..145

Caving...147

Technical Climbing...149

Resources...151

Also by the Author..153

About the Author...155

Index...157

Introduction

Exploring Great Basin National Park is a guide to both the national park and the adjacent Mount Moriah Wilderness. Although many visitors stay at the park for just a few hours, the purpose of this book is to encourage you to stay longer and explore the park as well as the nearby Humboldt-Toiyabe National Forest. You can camp at one of the four campgrounds in the park, camp on the national forest, or stay at a motel, hotel, or bed and breakfast in nearby Baker or Ely. If you are new to the area you should certainly take the tour of Lehman Caves and a drive up the Wheeler Peak Scenic Road. But these barely scratch the surface of this diverse area. Check out the opportunities for stargazing, bird watching, hiking, fishing, pine nut gathering, bicycling, horseback riding, picnicking, and more.

The area covered by this book lies within the Snake Range, which lies along the east-central Nevada-Utah border. The Snake Range is Nevada's second highest mountain range, culminating in 13,063-foot Wheeler Peak. US 50 crosses the Snake Range at Sacramento Pass, dividing the range into southern and northern sections. The South Snake Range features Wheeler Peak and Great Basin National Park, and the North Snake Range features the Mount Moriah Wilderness, crowned by its namesake peak, Mount Moriah at 12,067 feet.

Great Basin National Park was established in 1986 to preserve an outstanding section of the Great Basin. The park includes 77,100 acres in the South Snake Range. Great Basin National Park includes a remarkable diversity of landscapes: desert sagebrush flats, pinyon-juniper forests, pine-fir forests, subalpine forests, and alpine tundra. Lehman Caves, famous for its beautiful cave formations, is another attraction. Great Basin National Park features several well-maintained trails and a number of primitive trails which lead to a natural arch, several alpine lakes, the ancient bristlecone pine forests, and the top of Wheeler Peak. Much of the South Snake Range outside of the national park is managed by the Bureau of Land Management, including the Highland Ridge Wilderness Area south of the park.

The Mount Moriah Wilderness Area covers 82,000 acres in the North Snake Range. A unique feature of the wilderness is The Table, an 11,000 feet alpine plateau. The wilderness area offers an opportunity for solitude on infrequently traveled trails.

A good way to start your visit is at the Great Basin Visitor Center, located in Baker just outside the park. The visitor center features interactive exhibits that represent the entire Great Basin region.

Lehman Caves Visitor Center, at the end of the entrance road, provides the opportunity to learn more about the national park and nearby Lehman Caves. The Lehman Caves Visitor Center has maps and books, as well as an informative display on the park.

Jeff Davis Peak, also known as Doso Doyabi

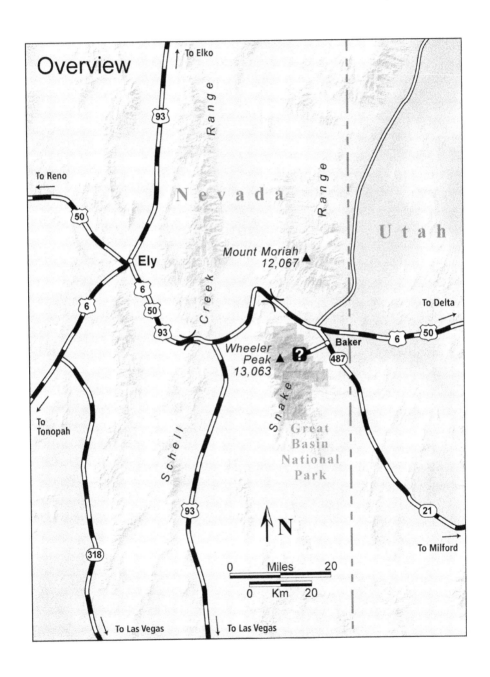

Overview

To Elko

93

To Reno

50

N e v a d a

Ely

6

50

93

6

6

Mount Moriah
12,067 ▲

Creek

Range

Range

U t a h

To Delta

Baker

487

To
Tonopah

Wheeler
Peak ▲
13,063

Snake

Schell

Great
Basin
National
Park

6   50

93

318

N

To Milford

21

Miles

0   20

0   Km   20

To Las Vegas   To Las Vegas

Park Updates

The park is making ongoing improvements to campgrounds and other facilities. Roads may be seasonally closed because of weather, wildfires, or roadwork. Before you visit, always check the park website, nps.gov/grba, for updates.

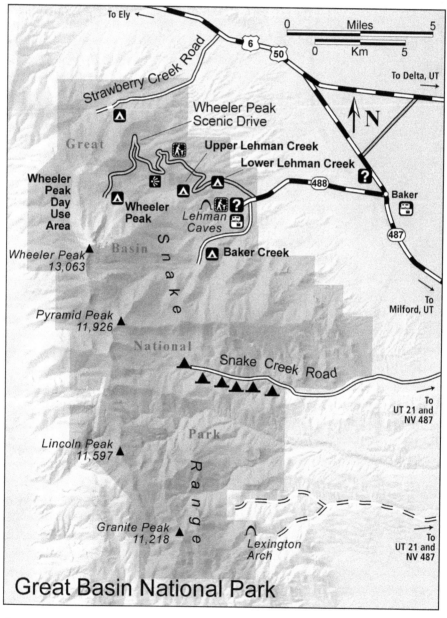

Great Basin National Park

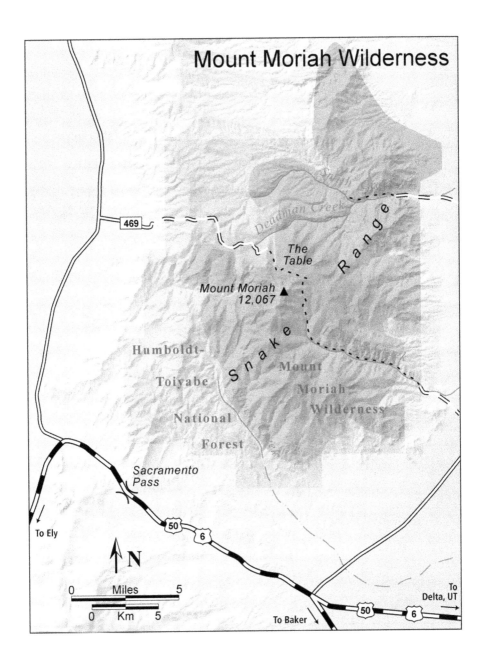

Mount Moriah Wilderness

Map Legend

)(	Pass	═══⟨17⟩═══	Interstate Highway
▲	Peak	══⟨89⟩⟨64⟩══	US/State Highway
⌐○	Spring	════════	Local Road
P	Parking	────────	Gravel Road
A	Campground	= = = = =	Unmaintained Road
🚮	Trailer Dump Site	- - - - - - - -	Featured Trail
▲	Primitive Campground	················	Cross-Country Route
⛱	Picnic Area	- - - - - - - -	Other Trail
?	Visitor Center	────────	River or Creek
👥	Ranger Station	── ── ── ──	Intermittent Stream
▪	Point of Interest		
✲	Viewpoint		

Ancient bristlecone pine

What is the Great Basin?

An elegant description of the Great Basin was written by geographer I.C. Russell in 1885:

> In the crossing from the Atlantic to the Pacific, between the Mexican boundary and the central portion of Oregon, one finds a region, bounded by the Sierra Nevada on the west and the Rocky Mountain system on the east, that stands in marked contrast in nearly all its scenic features with the remaining portions of the United States. The traveler in this region is no longer surrounded by the open, grassy parks and heavily timbered mountains of the Pacific slope, or by the rounded and flowing outlines of the forest-crowned Appalachians, and the scenery suggests naught of the boundless plains east of the Rocky Mountains or of the rich savannas of the Gulf States. He must compare it rather to the parched and desert areas of Arabia and the shores of the Dead Sea and the Caspian.

> The bare mountains reveal their structures almost at a glance, and show distinctly the many varying tints of their naked rocks. Their richness of color is sometimes marvelous, especially when they are composed of the purple trachytes, the deep-colored rhyolites, and the many-hued volcanic tuffs so common in western Nevada. Not infrequently a range of volcanic mountains will exhibit as many brilliant tints as are assumed by the New England hills in autumn. On the desert valleys the scenery is monotonous in the extreme, yet has a desolate grandeur of its own, and at times, especially at sunrise and at sunset, great richness of color. At mid-day in summer the heat becomes intense, and the mirage gives strange delusive shapes to the landscape, and offers false promises of water and shade where the experienced traveler knows there is nothing but the glaring plain. When the sun is high in the cloudless heavens and one is far out in the desert at a distance from rocks and trees, there is a lack of shadow and an absence of relief in the landscape that makes the distance deceptive- the mountains appearing near at hand instead of leagues away- and cause one to fancy that there is no single source of light, but that the distant ranges and the desert surfaces are self-luminous. The glare of the noonday sun conceals rather than reveals the grandeur of this rugged land, but in the early morning and near sunset the slanting light brings out mountain range after mountain range in bold relief, and reveals a world of sublimity. As the sun sinks behind the western peaks and the shades of evening grow deeper and deeper on the mountains, every ravine and cañon becomes a fathomless abyss of purple haze, surrounding the bases of gorgeous towers and battlements that seem encrusted with a mosaic more brilliant and intricate than the work of Venetian artists. As the light fades and the twilight deepens, the mountains lose their detail and become sharply outlined silhouettes, drawn in the deepest and richest purpose against a brilliant sky.

This region of unique topography covers about 200,000 square miles (500,000 square kilometers) and includes nearly all of Nevada, much of western Utah, and parts of California, Oregon, and Wyoming. Within this vast area, some 160 mountain ranges, all trending north-south, separate more than 90 valley basins. The term Great Basin refers to the fact that all of the drainage from the mountains flows into interior basins and none reaches the sea. A few of these basins include permanent lakes and some have seasonal lakes, but the majority of the valleys are dry. The mountain ranges tend to be long and narrow, from 30 to 120 miles long and 3 to 15 miles wide. Most ranges have peaks above 9,000 feet, and a dozen or so reach above 10,000 feet. The highest point is Boundary Peak, 13,140 feet, located in the White Mountains near the California border. Although the Great Basin is a desert, the higher mountains catch enough moisture from passing storms to support forests, streams, and lakes.

Weather and Climate

The Snake Range has a great variety of weather because of its great elevation range and also because of its interior continental location. In the high country, summer and autumn are the best hiking seasons. The lower desert areas are most enjoyable in spring and fall. In winter and spring, significant amounts of snow usually blanket the high country, and the peaks become the domain of the experienced winter mountaineer and backcountry skier. Elevations in the park range from 6,200 feet to 13,063 feet, a vertical range of almost 7,000 feet.

In the Great Basin, one view can encompass desert valleys to alpine tundra

During summer, the valleys commonly reach temperatures of 90°F during the afternoon and occasionally reach 100°F. Nights on the desert can be chilly, with temperatures dropping to 50°F or lower. The high country is the place to be in summer, with high temperatures around 75°F. Nights in the mountains can be cold, even in the summer, with temperatures dropping down to freezing. In the fall, daily high temperatures in the desert drop to an average of 75°F. Winter temperatures in the mountains can drop as low as -30°F, and occasionally reach subzero levels in the valleys as well.

The desert valleys and foothills receive about 10 inches of precipitation a year; the mountain crest may receive two or three times that amount. During the summer, most of the moisture comes as rain from sporadic thunderstorms. By late October, the weather shifts to a winter pattern and Pacific weather systems begin to reach the area. These storms bring snow to the mountains and rain to the valleys at first, but as winter approaches snow falls in the valleys as well. Winter storms dominate the weather through April. Deep snow usually lingers into May on the peaks, but the foothills and lower canyons are often snow-free in March.

Strong winds sometimes blow on the exposed ridges, and even during otherwise calm weather, the sharp temperature contrast at different elevations can cause strong up or down slope winds. This effect is especially noticeable in canyons and valleys.

Periods of stormy weather are interspersed with stretches of fine weather. Even in December and January more than half the days are either clear or partly cloudy. During summer and fall cloudy days are an uncommon treat. As in most mountain areas, the weather can change rapidly; snow falls every month of the year on the peaks and ridges, and thunderstorms in particular can build up quickly.

Summer thunderstorms often form over the mountains

History of the Snake Range

Prehistory

There is evidence that humans have occupied the Snake Range since about 9,000 to 12,000 B.C. These earliest people appear to have been small, mobile groups which spent their time hunting animals and gathering plants. They hunted big-game animals, such as mammoth, bison, camel, ground-sloth, and horse, which are now mostly extinct. Around 9,000 B.C., as the climate dried out, natives began to use a wider range of plant and animal products as food sources and for clothing and implements. Evidence survives in the form of manos and milling stones, baskets, moccasins, spears, and digging sticks. Some artifacts show that these people traded with coastal California. By 500 B.C., people in the Snake Range area had settled into a distinctive lifestyle, living part of the year in small villages and supplementing their diet with hunting and food gathering. These people developed a characteristic artistic style as expressed in their pottery and rock art. At the time of first European contact, the native American group occupying the area was known as the Western Shoshone. They lived in small villages near water sources and occupied small, conical brush houses. During the spring and summer, families dispersed to gather plant seeds and root and to hunt. In fall, the families held communal rabbit and antelope drives, and gathered pinyon pine nuts. By winter, groups of families would congregate in small villages in the pinyon-juniper zone along the lower slopes of the mountains.

Spanish Explorers

Extensive European exploration of North America began with the voyage of Columbus in 1492, but two hundred and fifty years later the Great Basin still lay uncharted and unknown. By the 1770's, Spain had established missions in California and New Mexico and was looking for an overland route to connect them. In 1776, the Garcés expedition explored the southern edge of the Great Basin, and the Escalante expedition reached a point about 80 miles east of the Snake Range.

Traders and Trappers

The next explorations of the Great Basin were done by British and American fur trappers such as Peter Skene Ogden and Jedediah Smith. Ogden was the first to explore the northern Great Basin, discovering the Humboldt River in 1829, which would later become the route of the Overland Trail. Smith was also the first to cross Sacramento Pass in the Snake Range in 1827. Driven by desire for profits in the lucrative fur trade and competition between British and American interests in western North America, other trappers rapidly completed the general exploration of the Great Basin by 1830.

Emigrant Trails

With the establishment of the Old Spanish Trail through the southern Great Basin, and the Overland Trail across the northern Great Basin, emigrants bound for California started to traverse the inhospitable desert. The trickle of parties in the early 1830's became a flood by 1850, spurred on by discovery of gold in California in 1849.

American Exploration

John Charles Frémont led several early expeditions to explore and map the west, and in 1844 discovered that the huge region between the Sierra Nevada and the Wasatch Mountains did not drain to the sea. He was the first to use the term 'Great Basin' to describe the area. After the Mormons successfully settled the Salt Lake Valley in Utah, they began to spread over a much wider region. Some of their outposts survived, others failed. In 1855, the White Mountain Mission expedition attempted to establish a settlement at present-day Garrison on the eastern slopes of the Snake Range. Snake Creek Farm, as it was called, lasted only three years. Meanwhile, the ongoing expedition produced the first written record of exploration in Great Basin National Park and was the first party to climb Wheeler Peak, known then as Jeff Davis Peak.

Transcontinental Routes

By 1850, the United States spanned the continent from coast to coast, and the government became interested in discovering practical routes across the Great Basin. In 1855, Howard R. Egan explored a route which crossed the northern end of the Snake Range. Captain James H. Simpson of the US Army was sent to the Great Basin in 1858 to do a reconnaissance of a more direct route to California and locate a site for a fort midway across the route. The Simpson expedition was the first scientific exploration and included a geologist, naturalist, photographer, and artist. During 1859-61, overland mail, stage, and telegraph service were begun along the Simpson-Egan route. The Pony Express was an ambitious express mail service which used this central route during 1860-61. It was quickly outmoded by the completion of the transcontinental telegraph. Further changes took place when the transcontinental railroad was completed along the Humboldt River in 1869 and most of the traffic moved to the swifter railroad.

Government and Private Surveys

After the turmoil of the American Civil War ended, the federal government sponsored a series of scientific surveys in the Great Basin. In 1869, George M. Wheeler was the leader of a reconnaissance survey of southern and southeastern Nevada, including the Snake Range. He and several of his men climbed the highest point in the Snake Range, which his men named Wheeler Peak in his honor. His report describes in detail the forests, wildlife, and mining in the Snake Range, as well as the native Americans. John Muir, the famous naturalist and conservationist, visited the Snake Range in the late 1870's in the course of his survey of the resources of Nevada's mountain ranges. He climbed Wheeler Peak and noted the evidence of glacial activity in the range. His journals and notebooks became the basis of his later articles and books calling for the protection of America's natural resources. In 1878, a new federal agency, the US Coast and Geodetic Survey, was given the task of completing precise survey measurements across the country. The Survey established triangulation stations on many of the Great Basin's highest summits. Using a transit-like instrument, the theodolite, the surveyors were able to take very accurate position measurements, which made it possible to accurately survey the land for legal boundaries and to produce accurate maps. Wheeler Peak was occupied for several seasons as part of this survey, and evidence of the survey station is still visible on the summit.

Miners and Loggers

Discovery of the Comstock Lode in 1859 in western Nevada set off the first mining rush in the Great Basin. When the Comstock Lode suffered a temporary depression in 1864, prospectors fanned out across the rest of Nevada. Discoveries were soon made in the Snake Range, but making a profit was difficult in the remote country. Miners have left their mark in every part of the range in the form of prospect holes and small shafts, but few sites were ever developed into large mines. Among the more notable operations in the South Snake Range were the Minerva tungsten mines, the Mount Washington copper-lead-antimony mines, and the St. Lawrence lead-silver mine on the southwest slopes, the Osceola placer gold mine on the northwest slopes, and the Johnson tungsten mine on the crest at Johnson Lake.

Logging has never been a major industry in the Snake Range because of the small forested area. In the past, timber was cut mainly to satisfy the needs of the mines and settlers. At one time there were lumber mills in South Fork Big Wash in the southern Snake Range and Hendrys Creek in the Mount Moriah area, among other sites.

Settlement

The population jump caused by the mining boom led directly to more permanent settlements. By 1869 a number of ranches and small farms had been established in the Spring Valley and the Snake Valley flanking the Snake Range. The settlers were dependent on the creeks flowing out of the mountains for their water supply and on the timber growing on the upper slopes for wood.

Well-known as the discoverer of Lehman Caves, Absalom S. Lehman established a ranch on a creek near the east boundary of the present-day national park in 1870. He discovered the cave in 1885, and exploration soon revealed the cave's beautiful and extensive natural decoration. He began to advertise the cave and serve as a guide, and by 1887 was establishing a new ranch at the cave to serve as a tourist center. He sold his old ranch on Lehman Creek in 1891, but died before he could develop his new ranch.

An Engelmann spruce growing in the ruins of Johnson Mine

The settlement of Baker was established by Ben Lehman (the brother of Absalom Lehman) and several others in the late 1870's. George W. Baker built a major cattle ranch at the town, which was later named for him. In 1911, the US Forest Service created a ranger station in Baker to administer the new Nevada National Forest, which included the Snake Range. Garrison was permanently settled about the same time as Baker by several families who began farming along lower Snake Creek.

The Snake and Spring Valleys have always been remote and difficult to reach by the standards of more populated regions. Railroad lines were extended to Ely, Nevada, and Milford, Utah by 1906, which helped ranchers and miners transport their products to market. US 50, the highway which crosses the Snake Range at Sacramento Pass, was completed by 1920 but not paved until 1947. Even today, the Snake Range is a long way from the nearest major cities.

Humboldt-Toiyabe National Forest

By 1880, conservationists such as John Muir and others were advocating preservation of the country's forests and natural wonders. Because of their work, the first national parks were established by 1890. In 1891, the National Forest Reserves were created, primarily to protect timber and watersheds. The US Forest Service was created in 1905 under the Department of Agriculture to administer the Forest Reserves, which were redesignated as National Forests in 1907. The present multiple-use and conservation policies of the Forest Service were largely developed by energetic Gifford Pinchot, the first Chief Forester. The Snake Range, including the future Great Basin National Park, was included in the Nevada National Forest created by President Theodore Roosevelt in 1909. As part of a major reorganization of the National Forests, the Nevada National Forest was eliminated in 1957, and the Snake Range became part of the Humboldt National Forest. More recently, the Humboldt and Toiyabe National Forests were combined into one administrative unit.

Lehman Caves National Monument

Cada C. Boak, a Tonopah mining broker and advocate of US Highway 50, led the effort, starting in 1920, to create a national monument at Lehman Caves. Two years later, President Warren Harding proclaimed Lehman Caves National Monument under the authority of the American Antiquities Act. The new monument was administered by the US Forest Service until 1933, when Lehman Caves and all other national monuments were transferred to the National Park Service under the Department of the Interior. In deference to grazing and mining interests, just one square mile was protected in the national monument.

Great Basin National Park

Shortly after the creation of the national monument, Boak and others began to advocate the idea of a national park in the Snake Range, but nothing came of these early efforts. Interest revived in 1955, primarily due to the efforts of Weldon F. Heald, who became interested in the Snake Range after his rediscovery of the

Wheeler Glacier on a five-day hiking trip. Partly because of the increasing public interest in preserving the South Snake Range as a scenic and recreational area, the US Forest Service designated the Wheeler Peak Scenic Area in 1959. As part of efforts to provide easy recreational access to the mountains, the US Forest Service built the Wheeler Peak Scenic Road and constructed several campgrounds in the mid 1960's. Over the years, several bills were introduced into Congress to create a Great Basin National Park, but none were passed. Strong opposition from ranching and mining interests was a major factor in the defeat of the park proposals. But by the mid-1980's, the movement to create a park revived. Mining and ranching were becoming less of an economic force and tourism was increasing. There was strong interest in protecting the remaining roadless areas in Nevada as part of the National Wilderness Preservation System, primarily by residents of the populous Reno and Las Vegas areas. This led to revived interest in a national park and much debate between local and national advocates and opponents as to the size and exact boundaries of the park. Finally, Congress passed a bill which President Ronald Reagan signed on October 27, 1986, creating the present 77,000-acre Great Basin National Park, Nevada's first national park.

The new national park inherited the facilities of the old Lehman Caves National Monument, including the small visitor center and the Forest Service campgrounds, roads, and trail system. As the new park became more well known and visitation increased, it soon became apparent that changes would have to be made in order to administer the area as a coherent national park. By 1992, a new general management plan was developed which called for the construction of a new entrance road and visitor center, and relocation and closure of some existing roads. Hikers would benefit from new hiking trails which would connect existing trails to form an expanded park-wide trail system.

Mount Moriah Wilderness

The Mount Moriah Wilderness protects 82,000 acres in the North Snake Range under the jurisdiction of the US Forest Service and the Bureau of Land Management. The Wilderness was created in 1989 as part of the Nevada Wilderness Act, which protected many roadless areas in the Humboldt-Toiyabe National Forests. Interest in protecting roadless areas began within the Forest Service in the 1930's, primarily under the influence of Aldo Leopold. The agency designated some places as wilderness closed to motorized travel, but these areas were protected only by administrative order. Wilderness advocates worked hard to gain more permanent protection for roadless areas, and their efforts resulted in the National Wilderness Preservation System created by Congress in 1964. The Wilderness Act immediately designated most of the existing National Forest Wilderness areas as part of the Wilderness System, but left a few areas to be administratively protected by the Forest Service as Primitive Areas. The Jarbidge Wilderness was the only designated wilderness area in Nevada before passage of the Nevada Wilderness Act. In wilderness areas, humans are intended to be temporary visitors. Permanent structures and motorized and mechanized vehicles, including bicycles, are kept out in order to preserve the primitive nature of the area. Mount Moriah Wilderness and the remainder of the Humboldt-Toiyabe National Forest within the Snake Range are presently administered by the Ely Ranger District, headquartered in Ely, Nevada.

The Snake Range was first protected as a National Forest Reserve in 1891

Getting to Great Basin National Park

Great Basin National Park and Mount Moriah Wilderness are located in east-central Nevada near the Utah border. Since there is no public transportation to or within the park area, you will need a car. US 50, the main east-west highway across central Nevada, bisects the north-trending Snake Range at Sacramento Pass. Great Basin National Park and the Highland Ridge Wilderness encompass a portion of the Snake Range south of US 50. Mount Moriah Wilderness, which is on the Humboldt-Toiyabe National Forest and Bureau of Land Management lands, encompasses part of the Snake Range north of US 50.

Nearby Towns

Baker is the nearest town, located on NV 487 five miles east of the park visitor center. Limited services are available. Ely is the largest city in the area, and is located at the junction of US 50 and US 93 about 67 miles northwest of the park. Full services are available. Cedar City, Utah, is 137 miles southeast of the park on I-15. Full services are available.

Airlines

Major airlines serve Las Vegas and Reno, Nevada, and Salt Lake City and Cedar City, Utah. Check www.kayak.com/flights for airlines and flights.

Bus

Greyhound Bus Lines serves Cedar City, Utah. www.greyhound.com, 800-231-2222.

Rental Cars

The nearest cities with rental cars are Las Vegas and Reno, Nevada, and Cedar City and Salt Lake City, Utah. All these cities have scheduled airline service.

Driving to the Park

From the west, via US 6-50, cross Sacramento Pass and then turn right on NV 487. Drive 4.9 miles south to the town of Baker, and then turn right on the park entrance road. Continue 5.3 miles to the Lehman Caves Visitor Center. (There is also a visitor center in Baker.)

From the north, via US 93 and US 50, cross Sacramento Pass and then turn right on NV 487. Drive 4.9 miles south to the town of Baker and then turn right on the park entrance road. Continue 5.3 miles to the Lehman Caves Visitor Center. (There is also a visitor center in Baker.)

From the east, via US 6-50, turn left on NV 487. Drive 4.9 miles south to the town of Baker and then turn right on the park entrance road. Continue 5.3 miles to the Lehman Caves Visitor Center. (There is also a visitor center in Baker.)

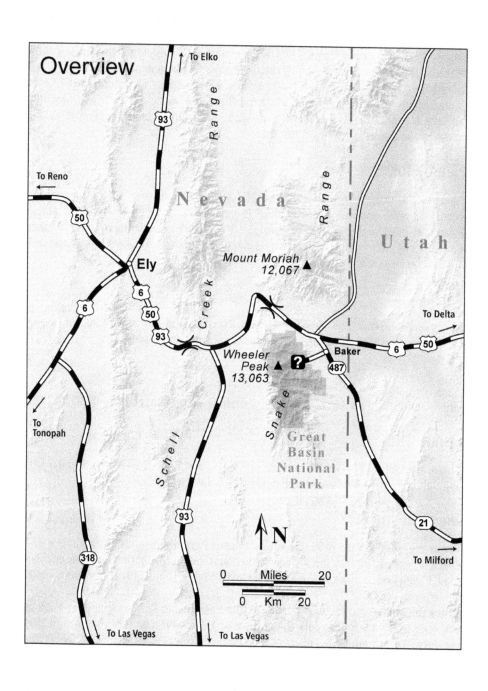

From the south, via US 93, turn right on US 6-50 and drive 30 miles, crossing Sacramento Pass, and then turn right on NV 487. Drive 4.9 miles south to the town of Baker and then turn right on the park entrance road. Continue 5.3 miles to the Lehman Caves Visitor Center. (There is also a visitor center in Baker.)

Getting Around the Park

Paved roads access a portion of Great Basin National Park, including the visitor centers, Lehman Caves, the Wheeler Peak Scenic Drive, and most of the campgrounds. Other areas, including the remainder of the park as well as Mount Moriah Wilderness, are accessible via graded and unmaintained dirt roads. This is very remote country- be prepared before venturing off paved roads. Make certain your vehicle is well-maintained and carry extra water, food, clothing, a first aid kit, and a flashlight. Cell phone coverage is spotty.

Some remote roads require a four-wheel-drive vehicle. These roads may not be passable to any vehicle after wet weather or during the winter. Such roads are noted in the text. Check with Great Basin National Park or the Humboldt-Toiyabe National Forest for current back road conditions.

- For current conditions in the park, check the park website: www.nps.gov/grba.

- For road conditions outside the park, check www.nvroads.com and udottraffic.utah.gov, or call 511.

Starting Your Visit

Entrance Fees and Passes

Great Basin National Park has no entrance fee. There is a fee for Lehman Caves Tours, for camping in the developed campgrounds and for the trailer dump site. Annual passes, such as the America the Beautiful Pass- The National Parks and Federal Recreational Lands Pass, do not cover cave tour, campground, or dump station fees. Holders of Golden Age and Golden Access Passes receive a discount on cave tours and campground fees but not on dump station fees.

Great Basin Visitor Center

This is the main park visitor center, and it is located just north of Baker on the west side of the highway. An information desk, exhibits, a theater, and bookstore will help you get started on your exploration of the park. The visitor center is open daily during the spring, summer, and fall, and is closed in winter. 775-234-7331 x 7520.

Lehman Caves Visitor Center

Located at the end of the park entrance road, 5.3 miles west of Baker, this is the starting place for guided tours of Lehman Caves. Plan ahead and reserve your tour at Recreation.gov. There are also exhibits, an information desk, a bookstore, and a nature trail.

Western National Parks Association Bookstores

WNPA operates bookstores in both park visitor centers, featuring books, maps, and other publications on the park and the Great Basin. They are open during regular visitor center hours. Contact them via www.wnpa.org, email grba@wnpa.org, or 775-234-7519.

Lehman Caves

Lehman Caves is one of the most highly decorated caves in the world

Touring Lehman Caves

Lehman Caves is named after Absalom Lehman, who settled nearby and discovered the cave in 1885. The cave, though small compared to famous caves such as Carlsbad Caverns, is highly decorated with cave formations and is well worth the visit. For the protection of these resources, all visits to the cave are guided by park rangers. Check at the Lehman Caves Visitor Center for walk times, fees, and advance ticket sales. Groups are limited to 20. Some of the cave passages are narrow; camera tripods and backpacks are not allowed. Sections of the trail through the cave may be wet and slippery since the path ascends and descends several sets of stairs. The cave temperature is 50F (10C) year round. Make advance reservations at www.Recreation.gov.

Scenic Drives

Wheeler Peak Scenic Drive is the only paved scenic road in the park. The Baker Creek Road is maintained gravel and is passable to passenger cars. Those with four-wheel-drive vehicles may want to drive the Strawberry Creek, Snake Creek Canyon, and Lexington Arch roads.

Points along the scenic drives are given in miles, starting from either the Lehman Caves Visitor Center, or Baker at the beginning of the park entrance road (NV 488 and NV 487.) Elevations are in feet.

Wheeler Peak Scenic Drive

Caution!

The Wheeler Peak Scenic Drive has a steep grade above Upper Lehman Creek Campground.

- Use lower gears, especially when descending

- Never stop in the roadway- it is extremely dangerous

- Always use pullouts

- Watch for deer and other animals that may suddenly run in front of your vehicle

- Single vehicles or trailers longer than 24 feet are prohibited beyond Upper Lehman Creek Campground because of the narrow road and lack of turnarounds

Life Zones

As you drive up the Wheeler Peak Scenic Drive, you will climb more than 3,000 feet and see a dramatic change in the plant life along the way. Plants and animals tend to form distinct communities, called life zones, within a range of elevations where the temperature and amount of moisture suits their needs. C. Hart Merriam developed the life zone concept while studying the distribution of plants and animals on the slopes of western mountains. On this drive, you will travel through life zones from sagebrush to near timberline.

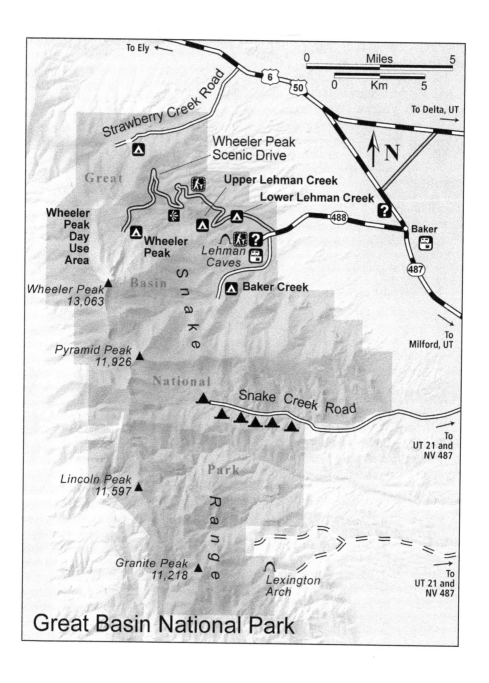

Great Basin National Park

Wheeler Peak from the scenic drive

0.0, 6,730: Leave the Lehman Caves Visitor Center and drive east on the park entrance road (NV 488.)

0.6, 6,825: Turn left on the Wheeler Peak Scenic Drive.

1.7, 7,000: Sage brush dominates the Great Basin Desert and some have referred to the region as a sea of sage. While there are many species of sage, the dominant plant is tall sagebrush, which is also Nevada's state flower. Sage grows from low elevations to timberline. To many people, the smell of sage, which is especially strong after a rain, symbolizes the American West.

3.1, 7,620: Upper Lehman Creek Campground is a common place to see mule deer grazing in the meadows near the creek. Mule deer are plentiful throughout the intermountain west and are named for their large, mule-like ears, which they use to listen for threatening predators. This is also the trailhead for the Lehman Creek Trail, a pleasant walk that follows Lehman Creek upstream to Wheeler Peak Campground. See Hike 4 for details.

4.3, 8,000: As you continue to climb, you enter pinyon-juniper woodland, or PJ for short. This forest of small trees is composed of juniper trees, which grow about 10 feet high, and pinyon pines, which are usually about 15 feet tall but may reach 30 feet in favored locations. Pinyon pines need slightly more moisture than junipers, so they favor north-facing slopes and somewhat higher elevations and become more common as you ascend through the PJ belt. Pinyon pines produce a tasty, nutritious nut, which was a staple food of native peoples and is still used today. The natives used juniper bark to make fibers used in sandals and mats, and the branches were used to make temporary shelters. Ranchers still use juniper logs for fence posts because they resist decay.

5.4, 8,400: Osceola Ditch. This 18-mile ditch was completed in 1885 and brought water from Lehman Creek on the east slopes of the mountains to the gold mines at Osceola on the western slopes. A short trail leads down to the remains of the ditch. For more information, see Hikes 1 through 3.

6.0, 8,600: Mount Moriah is visible to the north. At 12,050 feet, Mount Moriah is the highest summit in the North Snake Range.

6.9, 9,000: As you pass 9,000 feet, you are traveling through a beautiful forest of mixed conifers. Ponderosa pine, Douglas fir, and white fir are the main trees found here. Ponderosa pine has orange-ish bark and long needles which grow in clumps of three. Douglas fir is not a true fir, since its cones hang down. True firs such as white fir have cones that point upward from their branches. Both trees have flat needles that don't roll in your fingers.

7.4, 9,160: Mather Overlook is named for Stephen Mather, the first director of the National Park Service. The viewpoint overlooks Lehman Creek, which cascades from the alpine basin to the west past Upper and Lower Lehman Creek Campgrounds to the east.

10.3, 9,930: Wheeler View showcases the high point of the South Snake Range and the park, 13,063-foot Wheeler Peak, named for the leader of the government surveys. Wheeler Peak is the second-highest summit in Nevada. Jeff Davis Peak is the prominent peak to the left of Wheeler Peak. A small icefield below the precipitous north face of Wheeler Peak is the southernmost glacier in the northern hemisphere. The canyon containing the icefield is a glacial cirque, carved by much larger glaciers during ice age episodes. The last ice age ended about 10,000 years ago.

10.7, 10,000: Quaking aspen trees grace the mountainside. These deciduous trees have heart-shaped leaves attached by slender, flexible stalks, allowing the leaves to tremble in the slightest breeze. During the fall, aspens turn to beautiful shades of yellow, orange, and red, slashing entire mountainsides with bands of bright color. Groves of aspens tend to be the same color because they are actually one large cloned plant. In the west, aspens propagate by means of underground runners instead of seeds.

11.7, 10,160: Summit Trailhead is the starting point for the strenuous trail to the summit of Wheeler Peak, as well as a trail and cross-country hike to Bald Mountain. See Hikes 5 and 6 for details.

Quaking aspen turns brilliant red and gold during the fall

12.2, 9,800: Bristlecone Trailhead and Wheeler Peak Campground lie at the end of the road. A meadow in the lower portion of the campground offers views of the high peaks and is a fine place for a picnic before heading back down the mountain. From the trailhead, you can do an easy loop past two alpine lakes, take a trail to the ancient bristlecone forests and Wheeler Glacier or climb Wheeler Peak itself. See Hikes 5 through 8 for more information. At the lower end of Wheeler Peak Campground, you can descend a trail along Lehman Creek to Upper Lehman Creek Campground. See Hike 4 for details.

Baker Creek Road

The Baker Creek Road is a well-maintained gravel road that leads past Baker Creek Campground to Baker Trailhead. It is passable to passenger cars except when snow-covered.

0.0, 6,730: From the Lehman Caves Visitor Center, drive east 0.5 mile on the park entrance road (NV 488.)

0.5, 6,640 : Turn right onto the Baker Creek Road.

1.9, 7,072: Pass the turnoff to Gray Cliffs Group Campground and Pole Canyon Trailhead and Picnic Area on the left. Pole Creek Trail is a good hike to do when the higher elevations of the park are snow-covered, and the creekside trailhead is a great place for a picnic. See Hike 12 for details.

3.1, 7,620: Baker Creek Campground. See the Camping chapter for more information.

4.0, 8,000 feet: Baker Trailhead and the end of the road. This trailhead is the starting point for two strenuous but scenic trails which climb to remote alpine lakes nestled at timberline near the crest of the mountains. See Hikes 10 and 11 for details. If you aren't up to such long hikes, you can still take a stroll along the beginning of the South Fork Baker Creek Trail, which crosses Baker Creek on a footbridge. Watch for mule deer in this area, especially around dawn or dusk.

Strawberry Creek Road

This unmaintained road leads into Strawberry Creek at the north end of the South Snake Range. A four-wheel-drive vehicle is recommended.

0.0, 5,320: From Baker, drive northwest on NV 487.

5.0, 5,630: Turn left on US 6-50.

Krummholz trees are shaped by timberline winds

8.3, 6,062: Turn left on a signed, paved road which goes to a maintenance facility.

8.6, 6,088: Just before reaching the maintenance facility, turn right on the signed, unpaved road to Strawberry Creek.

10.5, 6,674: The road enters Strawberry Canyon and follows the creek to the southwest.

13.6, 7,905: Cross Strawberry Creek.

14.2, 8,196: The road ends in a scenic meadow with views of the peaks. There are several primitive campsites along the road, and two short hikes that can you do from this area- see Hikes 1 and 2.

Snake Creek Road

This unmaintained road follows Snake Creek into an aspen-lined meadow high on the east side of the South Snake Range, where there is a primitive campground and a trailhead. A four-wheel-drive vehicle is recommended.

0.0, 5,320: From Baker, drive southeast on NV 487.

5.2, 5,290: Turn right on Snake Creek Road, which begins as a maintained gravel road.

10.4, 6,250: The road enters Snake Creek Canyon and becomes unmaintained as it crosses the park boundary. There are several primitive campsites along this section. These pleasant sites next to Snake Creek are nice for camping and for picnicking.

17.2, 8,110: End of road at Johnson Lake Trailhead and Shoshone Primitive Campground set in an aspen grove next to the tumbling alpine creek. This is another fine place for a picnic. Sage meadows nearby have views of well-named Pyramid Peak. Several hikes, from easy to strenuous, start from this area. See Hikes 14 through 16.

Lexington Arch is a rare limestone arch

Lexington Arch Road

This unmaintained dirt road leads to the trailhead for Lexington Arch, a rare limestone arch, which is located in the southeast corner of the park. A high clearance vehicle is recommended. Please leave all gates as you find them to help keep livestock on their ranges.

0.0, 5,320: From Baker, drive southeast on NV 487, which becomes UT 21 after crossing the state line.

12.3, 5,380: Just past Pruess Lake, turn right on the Lexington Arch Road.

20.0, 6,410: The Lexington Arch Road enters Lexington Canyon.

21.5, 6.740: Stay left at a junction to remain on the Lexington Arch Road

22.4, 6,740: The road ends at the Lexington Arch Trailhead. A scenic trail leads to the limestone natural arch, which is not visible from the end of the road. See Hike 18 for more information. Most natural arches form in sandstone, but Lexington Arch is formed from limestone. It seems likely that the arch was once part of a cave system that eroded into the present arch.

Lodging and Services

In the Park

There is no lodging within the park.

Lehman Caves Gift Shop and Cafe

Open April to October, the cafe serves breakfast and lunch. The gift shop has souvenirs as well as camping and travel items. Bagged ice is also available. 775-234-7221.

Baker

T&D's Country Store, Restaurant, and Lounge

Open all year, the store offers groceries, ice, camping supplies, liquor, and fishing tackle. The restaurant serves lunch and dinner. The lounge is a full service bar with pool table and large screen TV. www.greatbasinxenman.com or 775-234-7264.

Stargazer Inn and Kerouac's Restaurant and Bar

Open late May through late October. The restaurant serves breakfast, lunch, and dinner. www.stargazernevada.com or 775-234-7323.

Great Basin Cafe

Serves breakfast and lunch. www.greatbasincafe.com or 775-234-7200.

Whispering Elms Motel, Campground & RV Park

Open April 1 through October 31. Offers 25 full service RV sites, 6 motel rooms, and large area for tents. Coin laundromat, showers, pool table, ice, fully stocked bar, and horseshoe pits. Camping supplies. www.WhisperingElms.com or 775-234-9900.

End of the Trail...er

Open May through October. This bed and bring-your-own-breakfast features two bedrooms (one queen, one twin) and a kitchenette. Enjoy a private deck with view of the Snake Range and Great Basin National Park, TV, telephone, and wireless Internet. No smoking. No pets. endofthetrailer.com or 775-234-7302.

Baker Sinclair Gas Station

Open year round. Self serve gas and diesel available 24 hours (credit or debit card required.) Laundromat, public restrooms, pay showers, and seasonal trail dump station.

Baker Post Office

Open year round. Full service U.S. post office. 775-234-7231.

Nearby

The Border Inn

Open year round. Located 8 miles northeast of Baker, on US Hwy 6&50 at the state line. Gas, diesel, ATM, motel, restaurant, bar, slots, pool table, video games, showers, dump station, phones, laundry, and souvenirs. Convenience store with ice. Offers 22 RV campsites with full hookups and pull-through spaces. Computer with Wi-Fi and printer. borderinncasino.com or 775-234-7300.

Hidden Canyon Retreat

Open year round. Located 15 miles south of Baker via NV 487 to Garrison, Utah. From the south end of Garrison, turn right (west) on a graveled road. Continue 6 miles to the ranch. Bed and breakfast in luxury lodge, or camping in teepees and cabins. Campsites, hot showers, recreation area, children's playground, heated pool, catch-and-release fishing, hiking, farm animals. Available for corporate retreats, church retreats, or family reunions. Reservations required. hiddencanyonretreat.com or 775-234-7172.

Picnicking

Lehman Caves Picnic Area

This picnic area near the Lehman Caves Visitor Center has several handicap-accessible sites with tables and fire grills. There are water and restrooms during the summer, and the area closes at sunset.

Upper Lehman Creek Picnic Area

This picnic area is located in Upper Lehman Creek Campground on the Wheeler Peak Scenic Drive. Picnic tables are available near the campground host site and near the amphitheater.

There is also a group picnic area that must be reserved at least two weeks in advance at Recreation.gov. The maximum group size is 75.

Mather Overlook

This overlook, about 8 miles up the Wheeler Peak Scenic Drive, has a picnic table, viewing telescope, and a restroom, and offers stunning views.

Bristlecone Trail Parking Area

Located at the end of the Wheeler Peak Scenic Drive, this site has several picnic tables and a restroom.

Pole Canyon Picnic Area

Located at the Pole Canyon Trailhead, just off the Baker Creek Road, this picnic area has several handicap-accessible sites with tables and fire grills. There is a restroom but no water.

Camping

There are four developed campgrounds in the park, and several primitive campgrounds with minimal facilities. All camping is first-come, first-served. Reservations are not accepted, except for the Gray Cliffs Group Campground.

There are no developed campgrounds in the Humboldt-Toiyabe National Forest encompassing the North Snake Range. There are several campgrounds on the national forest near Ely, in the White Pine and Schell Creek Ranges. See www.fs.fed.us/r4/htnf/ for more information. Dispersed camping is allowed on the national forest and on Bureau of Land Management lands, away from developed campgrounds. Respect all private property.

RV Dump Stations

A dump station is located 0.5 mile west of Baker on the park entrance road (NV 488.) This site also has water and trash receptacles. The dump station is normally open late May to October, weather permitting. There is a $5.00 fee.

There is also a dump station at The Border Inn, which is located 8 miles northeast of Baker on US Hwy 6&50 at the state line.

Showers

There are no showers in the park. Pay showers are available in Baker.

Lower Lehman Creek Campground

- Location: From the Lehman Caves Visitor Center, go 2.5 miles up the Wheeler Peak Scenic Drive.
- Season: All year
- Elevation: 7,300 feet
- Units: 11
- Tents: Yes
- RVs and Trailers: Yes, limited number of sites
- Dump Station: No
- Hookups: No
- Water: Summer only
- Showers: No
- Self-Serve Laundry: No
- Handicap-Accessible: Yes, one site
- Fee: $15.00 per night per site
- Management: Great Basin National Park, www.nps.gov/grba, 775-234-7331
- Reservations: None (first-come, first-served)

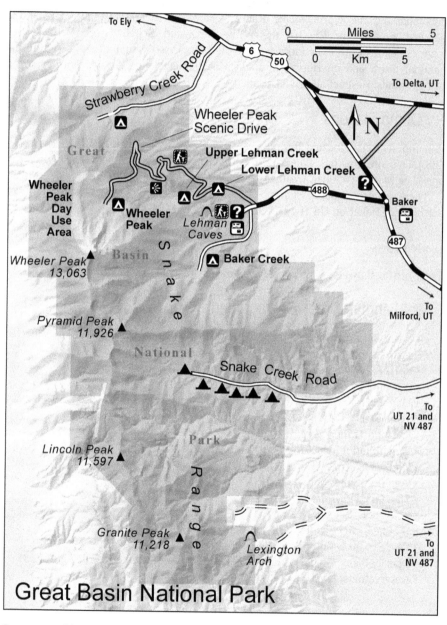

Campground locations in the park

Upper Lehman Creek Campground

- Location: From the Lehman Caves Visitor Center, go 3.5 miles up the Wheeler Peak Scenic Drive.
- Season: Mid-may through September
- Elevation: 7,750 feet
- Units: 22
- Tents: Yes
- RVs and Trailers: Yes, limited number of sites
- Dump Station: No
- Hookups: No
- Water: Yes
- Showers: No
- Self-Serve Laundry: No
- Handicap-Accessible: Yes, one site
- Fee: $15.00 per night per site
- Management: Great Basin National Park, www.nps.gov/grba, 775-234-7331
- Reservations: None (first-come, first-served)

Wheeler Peak Campground

- Location: From the Lehman Caves Visitor Center, go 14 miles to the end of the Wheeler Peak Scenic Drive.
- Season: June through September
- Elevation: 9,890 feet
- Units: 37
- Tents: Yes
- RVs and Trailers: Yes, limited to 24 feet on the Wheeler Peak Scenic Drive beyond Upper Lehman Creek Campground
- Dump Station: No
- Hookups: No
- Water: Yes
- Showers: No
- Self-Serve Laundry: No
- Handicap-Accessible: Yes, one site
- Fee: $15.00 per night per site
- Management: Great Basin National Park, www.nps.gov/grba, 775-234-7331
- Reservations: None (first-come, first-served)

Baker Creek Campground

- Location: From the Lehman Caves Visitor Center, go 3.0 miles up the graveled Baker Creek Road.
- Season: Mid-May through September
- Elevation: 7,530 feet
- Units: 34
- Tents: Yes
- RVs and Trailers: Yes
- Dump Station: No
- Hookups: No
- Water: Yes
- Showers: No
- Self-Serve Laundry: No
- Handicap-Accessible: Yes, one site
- Fee: $15.00 per night per site
- Management: Great Basin National Park, www.nps.gov/grba, 775-234-7331
- Reservations: None (first-come, first-served)

Grey Cliffs Group Campground

- Location: From the Lehman Caves Visitor Center, go 3.0 miles up the graveled Baker Creek Road.
- Season: Memorial Day to Labor Day
- Elevation: 7,120 feet
- Units: Four with 9 to 16 persons per site
- Tents: Yes
- RVs and Trailers: No
- Dump Station: No
- Hookups: No
- Water: No- water is available at nearby Baker Creek Campground and the RV Dump Site on the entrance road (NV 488)
- Showers: No
- Self-Serve Laundry: No
- Handicap-Accessible: No
- Fee: $15.00 per night for individual sites, $25 per night for group sites
- Management: Great Basin National Park, www.nps.gov/grba, 775-234-7331
- Reservations: Required, at Recreation.gov

Primitive Campsites

Within the park, there are several small, primitive campsites along Strawberry and Snake creeks which are accessible via back roads. These have picnic tables, and some have pit toilets. Water is not provided, but can be obtained at Lehman Caves Visitor Center and the RV Dump Station on the entrance road (NV 488.) There is no fee. Tents must be placed within 30 feet of the site's picnic table or fire ring. Generators are limited to the hours of 8:00 AM to 6:00 PM. Checkout time is noon and the stay limit is 14 days. Group site is limited to 15 persons, 6 pack animals, and 6 vehicles per site. RV's and trailers are not recommended.

Strawberry Creek

Strawberry Creek is in the northeast section of the park. From Baker, drive 5.0 miles northwest on NV 487, then turn left on US 6-50. Go 3.3 miles, then turn left on an unsigned, paved road which goes toward a maintenance facility. At 0.3 miles, just before reaching the facility, turn right on a signed dirt road to Strawberry Creek. There are several campsites along the road after it enters Strawberry Canyon, and a final campsite at the end of the road, 5.4 miles from US 6-50. The area is open year-round, but the access road can be muddy or snowy during winter.

Snake Creek

Snake Creek is in the southeast section of the park. From Baker, drive south 5.2 miles on NV 487, then turn right (west) on the signed, graded Snake Creek Road. There are several campsites next to Snake Creek after it enters Snake Creek Canyon, and Shoshone Primitive Campground is located in an aspen grove at the end of the road, 13 miles from NV 487. The area is open year-round, but the access road can be muddy or snowy during winter.

Commercial Campgrounds

Whispering Elms Motel, Campground & RV Park

Open April 1 through October 31. Offers 25 full service RV sites, 6 motel rooms, and large area for tents. Coin laundromat, showers, pool table, ice, fully stocked bar, and horseshoe pits. Camping supplies. www.WhisperingElms.com or 775-234-9900.

The Border Inn

Open year round. Located 8 miles northeast of Baker, on US Hwy 6&50 at the state line. Gas, diesel, ATM, motel, restaurant, bar, slots, pool table, video games, showers, dump station, phones, laundry, and souvenirs. Convenience store with ice. Offers 22 RV campsites with full hookups and pull-through spaces. Computer with Wi-Fi and printer. borderinncasino.com or 775-234-7300.Hidden Canyon Ranch Located 15 miles south of Baker via NV 487 to Garrison, Utah. From the south end of Garrison, turn right (west) on a graveled road. Continue 6 miles to the ranch. A main lodge, cabins, RV camping, and tent sites are available. www.hcr-nv.com/, 775-234-7172.

Hidden Canyon Retreat

Open year round. Located 15 miles south of Baker via NV 487 to Garrison, Utah. From the south end of Garrison, turn right (west) on a graveled road. Continue 6 miles to the ranch. Bed and breakfast in luxury lodge, or camping in teepees and cabins. Campsites, hot showers, recreation area, children's playground, heated pool, catch-and-release fishing, hiking, farm animals. Available for corporate retreats, church retreats, or family reunions. Reservations required. hiddencanyonretreat.com or 775-234-7172.

Pyramid Peak from near the Shoshone Primitive Campground at the end of the Snake Creek Road

For Kids and Families

I am glad I shall never be young without wild country to be young in. Of what avail are 40 freedoms without a blank spot on the map? -Aldo Leopold

Family activities at Great Basin National Park include ranger-led talks and hikes, the WebRanger program, and the Junior Ranger program. For current information on ranger programs, download the park newspaper, www.nps.gov/grba/parknews/newspaper.htm

The Alpine Lakes Trail

Starting from the Bristlecone Trailhead at the end of the Wheeler Peak Scenic Drive, the Alpine Lakes Trail loops through cool alpine forest and past two alpine lakes. There is plenty to explore along the way, and there are awesome views of the mountains, so bring lunch and make a day of it.

Be a WebRanger!

If you have access to the Internet, you can become a National Park WebRanger by going to www.nps.gov/kids/webrangers.htm, even from home before or after your visit to Great Basin National Park. You can play more than 50 games, learn about the national parks, and share park stories and pictures with other WebRangers around the world.

Junior Ranger Programs

Junior Rangers have fun learning about Great Basin National Park and the Snake Range, and represent the park to their friends and families. There are a few things you need to do so that you can become a Junior Ranger of Great Basin National Park, and all are free of charge.
   1. Attend one of these four programs:
     • Lehman Caves Tour
     • Campground Evening Program
     • Night Sky Program
     • A Ranger Talk
   2. Complete the appropriate number of activities in the Great Basin National Park and Lehman Caves Junior Ranger booklet for your age. Booklets are available at any park visitor center:
     • 5 and under- three activities
     • 6 to 9- five activities
     • 10 and up- seven activities
After completing these activities, show your booklet to a park ranger and receive a Junior Ranger Badge!

Teresa Lake on the Alpine Lakes Trail, which is easily accessible to families with children via an easy walk

Photography

The virtue of the camera is not the power it has to transform the photographer into an artist, but the impulse it gives him to keep on looking - and looking.
-Brooks Atkinson

Because Great Basin National Park is so far from the nearest large cities, most visitors arrive during the middle of the day and spend just a few hours in the park. Especially during the summer, the sun is high in the sky and floods the mountains with harsh light that washes out colors. For better outdoor photography, camp at the park or stay in a lodge and shoot early and late in the day, when the light is softer and colors more brilliant.

How to Shoot

It's Not Your Equipment

Though the features on pro or semi-pro single lens reflex cameras are designed for versatility and flexibility in many different shooting situations, you can make stunning photographs with modest equipment, as long as you understand its limitations. Point and shoot cameras, as well as the cameras built into smart phones, have remarkably good lenses, thanks to computer-aided design.

Seeing the Light

The human eye is a remarkable instrument. It is far more sensitive to light than any camera, and also has an extremely sophisticated processor- the brain. The brain processes what we see into what we expect to see, based on what we've already experienced. This means we don't see the strong blue cast to the midday light on someone's face, caused by the strong blue light from the open sky. Focused on the towering peak dominating the frame, we miss the that scraggly tree branch sticking into our picture.

Composition in Thirds

The placement of objects within your photo should create a pattern that is pleasing to the eye and draws the viewer into the image. Remember the rule of thirds, which states that major objects such as people, trees, rock formations, or the horizon should be placed one-third of the way in from the edge of the frame, rather than in the center. Centered subjects make for dull photos. Action subjects such as hikers or cyclists should be positioned at the one-third point and should be moving into the remaining two-thirds of the frame. In other words, give them space.

Simplify

When composing your shot, eliminate distractions and include as little in the frame as you can and still tell the story that you're trying to convey to your viewers. Move closer to your subject or use a telephoto lens or setting. Watch out for wide-angle lenses or settings. Used carefully, wide-angle lenses can create breathtaking images that sweep the viewer from intimate detail in the foreground to broad landscapes in the background, but they can also be loaded with irrelevant clutter.

Golden Light

Experienced landscape photographers know about the golden hours, the hour after sunrise and the hour before sunset when the sun is low to the horizon and the light is filtered by the atmosphere into soft, warm tones. Mountains leap into three dimensions and seem to glow with inner fire. Shadows and haze fill the canyons and add an aura of mystery.

During the summer, you'll have to rise early, or stay out late, to catch the golden hours. During the spring and fall, when the days are shorter, it's less work to get out during the golden hours. And even the mid-day light is softer due to the lower sun angle. Winter light is often stunning all day, especially as a storm clears.

The Photographer's Ephemeris (http://app.photoephemeris.com) is a map-based app that helps you plan your photography around sunrise and sunset times and the point on the horizon where the sun will rise and set. Also available as an app for iPhone and Android, it has many other functions, including moon rise and set, and rise and set times adjusted for a high horizon.

Where to Shoot

If your time is limited, drive the Wheeler Peak Scenic Drive. There are several viewpoints along the way, and a short walk along the Alpine Lakes Trail (Hike 7) will give you numerous opportunities for stunning shots.

If you have more time, drive the Baker Creek road to Baker Campground. If you have a high-clearance, four-wheel-drive vehicle, drive the Snake Creek and Lexington Arch Roads. Lexington Arch (Hike 18) is a definite photographic challenge.

Backcountry

Limiting your photography to places accessible by car or truck barely scratches the potential of this park. To really explore the area photographically, you have to explore it physically, which means hiking the trails. In the park, the Alpine Lakes Trail, Bald Mountain, Wheeler Peak, and Bristlecone-Glacier Trail (Hikes 5 through 8) offer superb scenery and many opportunities for photography.

Mount Moriah and The Table, in the Mount Moriah Wilderness, are remote areas far off the beaten track that are great to explore with a camera. The Table has a forest of gnarled, ancient bristlecone pines. The easiest hike to this area is the Big Canyon Trail (Hike 21), though you do need a four-wheel-drive vehicle to reach the trailhead.

Wheeler Peak glows at sunrise

Camera Gear for Hiking and Backpacking

On long hikes where weight becomes critical, you can't carry much photo gear. A waterproof point-and-shoot digital camera with a wide range zoom lens makes a great backpacking camera. Or you can carry a lightweight single lens reflex (SLR) camera body (these are often classed as semi-pro cameras) and two lenses- a wide-angle zoom and a telephoto zoom. Another option is a mirrorless interchangable lens camera, which is lighter and more compact than an SLR but still lets you change lenses. Some of these cameras are moisture and dust-sealed, a valuable feature for the outdoor photographer.

Batteries and Storage Cards

Unless you'll have access to a charger and a computer or image storage device every day, make certain you have enough memory cards and fully charged batteries to last the trip. Memory cards are inexpensive, so there's no excuse for running out of space. Camera batteries are still relatively expensive, but current digital cameras use far less power than the early models. You can greatly extend battery life by turning off the LCD monitor and using the optical viewfinder, if your camera has one. Also, turn off instant review and use the play button to selectively review photos as needed. When camping, resist the urge to edit your photos on the camera, unless you have a solar panel or some other way to recharge or replace the batteries.

Commercial Photography

In the park, commercial photography or videography involving props, models, professional crews and casts, or set dressings requires a permit. Personal or professional photography involving no more than a tripod and that doesn't disrupt other visitors does not require a permit or a fee in any national park. But note that tripods are not allowed on the Lehman Caves tour because of the tight passages.

Wildflower Viewing

The elevation range and different life zones in the Snake Range provide habitat for hundreds of flower species. Although there are always flowers to be seen during spring and summer, the wildflower display varies greatly from year to year, depending largely on the amount and timing of winter and spring precipitation. Early in the season, there will be more flowers at lower elevations. Later in the season, flowers will be more common at higher elevations. Although flowers can be found throughout the Snake Range, several locations stand out.

Wheeler Peak Scenic Drive

The Wheeler Peak Scenic Drive is a good place to look for summer wildflowers. Early in the summer, watch for evening primrose and desert mallow. Later on, look for paintbrush, golden peas, and penstemon. Prickly poppies flower throughout the summer.

Alpine Lakes Trail

A walk around the easy Alpine Lakes Trail (Hike 7) is a good way to view alpine wildflowers. Because of the short growing season above 10,000 feet, flowers in this environment are smaller and lower to the ground. Look for mountain bluebells, Jeffry's shooting stars, Parry's primrose, and crimson columbine.

Baker Creek Trail

A harder hike but worth it for the flowers alone, the Baker Creek Trail (Hike 10) climbs nearly 2,000 feet along Baker Creek. During late spring, you'll walk through fields of golden arrowleaf balsamroot. Wild rose is common, and manzanita will bear hundreds of tiny pink lantern-shaped flowers. In the summer, watch for sego lilies and paintbrush in open areas and yellow monkey flowers, shooting stars, monkshood, clover, parsley, and white bob orchids near Baker Creek. Other flowers include bluebells, harebells, fleabane, yellow columbine, blue-eyed mary, lupine, and prickly pear cactus.

Alpine phlox on the slopes of Bald Mountain

Bird Watching

Because of the great elevation range, 6,000 to over 13,000 feet, the Snake Range is an ideal place to observe birds. There are a great variety of habitats, from sage brush to arctic-alpine. Some birds such as the pinyon jay are associated with a specific habitat- in this case, the pinyon-juniper woodland found at intermediate elevations. The pinyon jay is completely dependent on pinyon pine nuts. Other birds, such as the common raven, are found in many different habitats because they are versatile eaters.

The park encourages birders to report uncommon or previously unknown birds. Ask for a copy of the current park bird checklist at either visitor center.

Clark's Nutcracker- Wikipedia Commons

Birds to Watch in the Park

The easiest way to travel through much of the range of habitats the Snake Range has to offer is to drive from Baker up the Wheeler Peak Scenic Drive. You can also drive the Baker Creek Road. Hikers can travel through many of the same habitats on the park trail system and in the Mount Moriah Wilderness, and can also climb higher to the timberline forests and alpine tundra.

Baker Area

Here, in sagebrush and grasslands, watch for bald eagles and hawks on telephone poles and wires. Red-tailed hawks like to sit on fence posts. During summer dusk or dawn, stop and listen for the whinnying of common snipe, the call of a common poor-will, the "whooo" of a Great Horned Owl, or the "bull-bat" roar of a Common

Nighthawk. At night, watch for the "copper-penny-colored" eye of the poor-will reflecting in your headlights.

- Long-billed curlew
- Northern harrier
- Golden eagle
- Killdeer
- Northern harrier
- Golden eagle
- Common raven
- American kestrel
- Song sparrow
- Red-tailed hawk
- Scrub jay
- California quail
- Eurasian chukar
- Sage grouse
- Mourning dove
- Horned lark
- Scrub jay
- Black-billed magpie
- Western kingbird
- Barn swallow
- Loggerhead shrike
- Black-throated sparrow
- Cassin's finch
- European starling
- Red-winged blackbird
- Western meadowlark

Pinyon-Juniper Woodland

On the Wheeler Peak Scenic Drive above Upper Lehman Creek campground, as well as around the Lehman Caves Visitor Center, look for

- Mountain chickadee
- Broad-tailed hummingbird
- Black-chinned hummingbird
- Rufous hummingbird
- Pinyon jay
- Mountain bluebird
- Solitary vireo

- Say's phoebe
- White-crowned sparrow

Lower Lehman Creek Campground

Along Lehman Creek, and also and also along Baker Creek near Baker Creek Campground, you may see
- American dipper
- Mountain chickadee
- Yellow-rumped warbler
- Cassin's finch
- Broad-tailed hummingbird
- Black-chinned hummingbird
- Mountain bluebird
- Western tanager
- Black-headed grosbeak

Upper Lehman Creek Campground

In the ponderosa pine forest along Lehman Creek, watch for
- Violet-green swallow
- Red-naped sapsucker
- Downy woodpecker
- Hairy woodpecker
- Mountain chickadee
- Bushtit
- White-breasted nuthatch
- House wren
- Warbling vireo
- Yellow-rumped warbler
- Black-headed grosbeak
- Chipping sparrow
- Green-tailed towhee
- Rufous-sided towhee
- Dark-eyed junco
- Brown-headed cowbird

Wheeler Peak Campground

In the aspen and limber pine forest and along the Alpine Lakes Trail, you may spot
- Clark's nutcracker
- Stellar's jay
- Townsend's solitaire

- Mountain chickadee
- Bushtit
- Yellow-rumped warbler
- Pine siskin
- Brown creeper
- Pygmy nuthatch
- Cooper's hawk
- Red crossbills

Alpine Lakes Trail

A hike around this easy loop past the two alpine lakes may reveal some of the waterbirds that pass through the area:

- Great blue heron
- Canada geese
- Sandhill crane
- Mallard
- Green-winged teal
- Northern pintail
- Northern shoveler
- Cinnamon Teal

Bristlecone-Glacier Trail

At timberline, in the ancient groves of bristlecone pines, look for

- Black form of rosy finch
- Rock wren
- Common raven
- Clark's nutcracker

Star Gazing

The Snake Range is far from major population centers and the high elevation skies are clear and dry much of the time. As a result, the area has some of the darkest skies in the United States, perfect for enjoying the glories of the universe.

Where to Go

Choose a location that is open and away from artificial light. Two of the best spots in the park are the meadow at the lower end of Wheeler Peak Campground and Mather Overlook along the Wheeler Peak Scenic Drive. Outside the park, the Baker Archaeological Site, just outside Baker, has a view that is unobstructed from horizon to horizon. Backpackers can pick from sites that are even farther from man-made lights. The Table in the Mount Moriah Wilderness is an absolutely stunning place to camp under starlit skies. Johnson and Baker Lakes lie at timberline, and though the horizon is slightly constricted by the surrounding peaks, the view of the sky is enhanced by the mountains. See Hikes 10 and 11, Hike 14, and Hikes 20 and 21. When you arrive on site, especially if you drove or used a flashlight to find your way, allow 20 minutes for your eyes to adjust to the dark. This is especially important when looking at a meteor shower.

Night sky and bristlecone pine- National Park Service

When to Go

Although you can look at the stars any time of the year, winter nights can be bitterly cold. Spring, summer, and fall are the best times of the year. Watch the weather forecast and pick a night that is predicted to be clear. Even high clouds dim the stars. Seeing individual stars and other objects is best on nights with a new moon, because a bright moon washes out faint objects. On the other hand, a night with a full or nearly full moon is good for learning the major constellations, as the dimmer stars are hidden and the constellations stand out more.

Moon Phase Calculator

www.stardate.org/nightsky/moon/

What to Bring

- Warm clothing, gloves, and hat
- Thermos with a hot drink
- A blanket, ground cloth, or reclining camp chair
- Binoculars- even small backpacking binoculars will review many more stars and sky objects
- Star chart- available at the park bookstores
- Red-lensed flashlight to protect your night vision. You can cover a white lens with red paper.

What to Look For

Use a star chart to orient yourself to the sky and see what is above the horizon at the present date and time.

Milky Way

The Milky Way is a faint band of light across the entire sky composed of millions of stars that are too faint to see with the naked eye. These stars make up the Milky Way Galaxy, of which our Sun is a member star. When you're looking at the Milky Way, you are literally looking at our home galaxy edge-on.

Constellations

From ancient times, humans have found patterns in the stars. Today, 88 constellations are recognized, covering the entire sky. All stars and other objects are found within one of these constellations, which in modern usage define a precise region of the sky. About half the constellations are major, made up of bright stars in a easily recognizable pattern. Learning the major constellations is the first step to knowing your way around the night sky. A few of the major constellations to look for during a summer night around 9 PM:

Ursa Major, the Great Bear: Look north to find the "Big Dipper," a group of stars that make up a dipper hanging from its handle with the bowl pointing right. The Big

Dipper is an asterism- a named group of stars within the Great Bear constellation. The lower two stars of the dipper are the "Pointer Stars." A line drawn to the right through the pointer star passes through Polaris, the North Star. In turn, the North Star forms the end of the handle of the "Little Dipper", part of the constellation Little Bear. The Little Dipper is much smaller and fainter than the Big Dipper.

Cassiopeia: To the right and below the North Star is a bright group of stars forming a sideways "W" in the sky.

Lyra: Nearly overhead in the summer sky, Lyra is a small but bright constellation representing a lyre, an ancient musical instrument. A nearly perfect triangle shares one star with a parallelogram. The very bright star at one point of the triangle is Vega, one of the brightest stars in the sky.

Sagittarius, the Archer: In the southern sky, near the horizon, look for a group of bright stars forming an almost-perfect teapot, complete with handle, lid, and spout.

Scorpius, the Scorpion: Just to the right of Sagittarius, a large group of stars looks like a huge scorpion, with a bright pair of stars on the left making up the stinger, and a small group of fainter stars on the upper right representing the head. The bright red star in the middle of the constellation is Antares, a giant red star that is the heart of the scorpion.

Meteors

Meteors, or "shooting stars," are small pieces of rock that enter our atmosphere from space at tremendous speeds. The streak of light is the object burning up in the atmosphere. Most meteors are the size of a speck of sand, but occasionally a larger one will create a spectacular "fireball" in the sky, bright enough to light up the ground around the observer. Most meteors are natural objects, but occasionally you may spot pieces of a man-made satellite burning up in the atmosphere. You can tell the difference by the color- natural meteors are yellow, orange, or red, while artificial objects are usually bluish or greenish.

Meteor showers appear at certain times of the year and the show may include dozens or even hundreds of meteors per hour. The best meteor showers are the Perseids in August, the Orionids in October, the Leonids in November, and the Geminds in December.

Major meteor showers

www.amsmeteors.org/showers.html

Planets

Five planets are visible to the naked eye- Mercury, Venus, Mars, Jupiter, and Saturn. Even small binoculars will show you the phases of Venus, the red color of Mars, the moons of Jupiter, and the rings of Saturn. Because the planets orbit the Sun at various speeds, they appear to move across the sky, but always along the Ecliptic, the plane of the solar system.

Planet finder

www.lightandmatter.com/planetfinder/en/

Satellites

There are thousands of artifical satellites orbiting the earth, and many are easily seen by the naked eye. The best time to observe satellites is just after dusk, when the observer is in the dark but sunlight still strikes the satellites high overhead. Lie on your back and let your gaze wander over a broad patch of sky, looking for a "star" that moves. Some satellites, such as the Iridium series and the International Space Station, are very bright and are in low orbits that cause them to move quickly across the sky.

Satellite Information:

Heavens Above is a good Web site for satellite information: www.heavens-above.com

Pine Nut Gathering

Pine nut gathering is a Great Basin tradition that started with the native peoples and is popular today as a great way to harvest an especially tasty food. In the Snake Range, pine nuts are harvested from the singleleaf pinyon, Pinus monophylla, which grows in mixed stands with Utah juniper between 6,000 and 9,000 feet. It is the only North American pine with single needles. All other pines have needles in bunches of two or more.

Pinyon pine- Wikipedia Commons

Pine nut gathering in Great Basin National Park is allowed only during the fall. To minimize impact to the park and ensure that plenty of food remains for Clark's nutcrackers, pinyon jays, and ground squirrels, please observe the following park rules:

- Pinyon pine nuts may be gathered and removed from the park only for personal non-commercial use.

- Limits are: 25 lbs per household per year or three gunnysacks of cones per household per year.

- When laid flat, each gunnysack must be no larger than two feet by three feet. Those found in possession of pine nuts or cones in excess of these amounts may be cited and the pine nuts and cones will be confiscated. Parking is allowed only in gravel or paved parking areas.

- Do not drive or park off-road. All-terrain vehicles and other off-road vehicles are strictly prohibited. Breaking branches, cutting, pulling, shaking, climbing, or otherwise injuring pines or other plants is illegal.

- Only free standing ladders may be used for picking.

Fishing

Fishing Regulations

Nevada state fishing regulations, www.nps.gov/grba/planyourvisit/fishing-regulations.htm, apply in Great Basin National Park, on the Humboldt-Toiyabe National Forest, and on BLM and state lands. A Nevada state fishing license is required for those 12 years of age or older. An annual license also requires a trout stamp.

Worms are permitted, but all other live bait, including amphibians and non-preserved fish eggs is prohibited in the park. Fishing is by rod and reel only. Catch-and-release fishing with barbless hooks is encouraged.

Locations to Fish

The Snake Range Recreational Fishing brochure is available at the visitor centers. The brochure includes a map of the North and South Snake ranges, and features full color fish illustrations.

- Lehman Creek: From Upper Lehman Creek Campground to the park boundary- brown, brook, and rainbow trout
- Baker Creek: From Baker Creek Trailhead through Grey Cliffs Group Campground- brown, brook, and rainbow trout
- Snake Creek: From park boundary to pipe inlet- brown and brook trout
- Strawberry Creek: Catch-and-release Bonneville cutthroat trout
- Baker Lake: Reached via Baker Creek Trail (see Hike 10.) Baker Lake, elevation 10,730 feet, is about four acres and the level drops steadily through the summer. Brook and Lahontan cutthroat trout.
- Johnson Lake: Reached via Baker Creek or Johnson Lake trails (see Hike 10 and Hike 14.)
- Shingle and Williams creeks: Reached by four-wheel-drive roads on the west side of the park- Brook and Lahontan cutthroat trout

Whirling Disease

This disease causes fish to be deformed and swim in tight circles. Whirling disease is currently expanding into Utah and northern Nevada, but is not present in Great Basin National Park. Please help keep it out by following these regulations:

- Moving live fish between bodies of water is prohibited in the park. Doing so can aid in the spread of disease.

- Thoroughly wash all waders and other gear before entering a different creek or body of water.

- If you have previously fished in an area that contains whirling disease, clean your gear, including boots and waders, with a 10% bleach solution. Let them dry in the sun to kill any spores before fishing in the park.

Johnson Lake

Horseback Riding

Wild horses- Wikipedia Commons

Horses and pack animals, including mules, burros, and llamas, are welcome in the backcountry of Great Basin National Park.

- Horses are not allowed in developed campgrounds.

- Camping at trailheads is prohibited.

- Horses and pack animals are prohibited on paved roads, in campgrounds and developed areas (picnic areas, visitor center areas), on self-guided interpretive trails, and in day use zones.

- Horses and pack animals are allowed on all trails except: Wheeler Peak Day Use Area trails, Osceola Ditch trail, Lexington Arch trail, and Baker to Johnson Lake Cutoff trail. Portions of trails may close to horse and pack animal use for safety or environmental concerns.

- Up to 6 horses or pack animals are allowed per group for day or overnight use. Larger groups may request an exception to these limits from the Superintendent under the terms of a Special Use Permit.

- Manure piles dropped at trailheads or in overnight backcountry camping areas must be scattered.

- All feed must be certified "weed free." Please remember to use weed-free feed for one week prior to arrival. This helps to reduce the spread of noxious weeds.

- Do not tie animals to trees or other vegetation for more than 60 minutes or in a manner that causes damage to park resources.

- Do not picket, hobble, or allow animals to graze within 100 feet of any lake, stream, spring, or riparian area.

- Horses or pack animals may not be tied to or secured within historic structures such as cabins, mills or corrals.

- Horse trailers may not be cleaned out in the park.

Pack trips must follow the Backcountry Guidelines on page 65.

Certified Weed-Free Hay is Required

All hay and straw entering national parks and national forests must be Certified Noxious Weed-Free. Animals must be fed Certified Noxious Weed-Free hay for one week prior to arrival. Visitors will be required to show proof of certification for all hay or straw used while in the park. Visitors using uncertified hay or straw will be fined. The intent is to reduce the spread of non-native, invasive weeds on Federal land.

For more information:

www.trailmeister.com/what-is-weed-free-feed-and-why-does-it-matter/

Ben Roberts at Great Basin National Park: 775-234-7331
Dave Palmer or Chandler Mundy at the Forest Service: 775-289-3031
Bob Wilson at the County Extension Office: 775-289-4459
Dawn Rafferty at Nevada Department of Agriculture: 775-688-1182

Bicycling

Bicycling is allowed on paved and dirt roads in the park, but not on trails. On the Humboldt-Toiyabe National Forest and BLM lands, bikes are allowed on trails and roads, except where designated to the contrary. Bikes are not allowed on trails within the Mount Moriah Wilderness. For descriptions of the following rides, see the Scenic Drives chapter.

Suggested Rides

Wheeler Peak Scenic Drive

This scenic, paved road is a good road ride. Use caution for heavy traffic during the summer and fall.

Strawberry Creek Road

This two-track road into the northeast corner of the park is a pleasant mountain bike ride with a gradual climb.

Snake Creek Road

Partially maintained, the Snake Creek Road follows Snake Creek to end at a primitive campground set in an aspen grove.

Lexington Arch Road

Another road that is partly maintained and partly two-track, the road to Lexington Arch Trailhead climbs up a scenic canyon enroute.

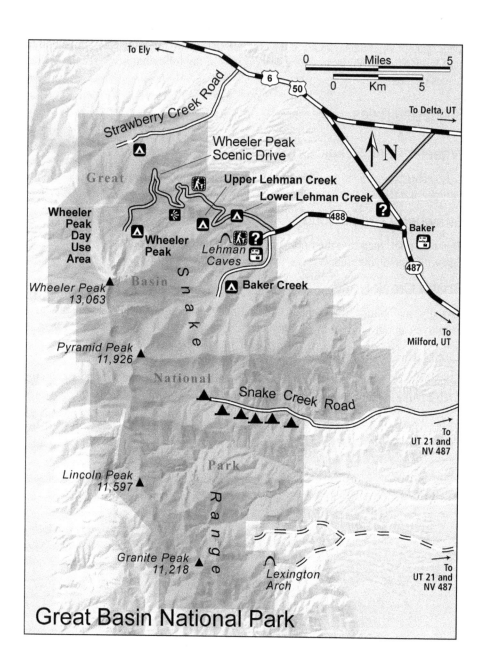

Great Basin National Park

Hiking

The best-kept secret of Great Basin National Park is its incredible backcountry. If you would like to hike through stands of ancient trees as old as civilization, to walk along a cascading mountain creek, to camp in a cool mountain forest, or to hike a high ridge with 100-mile views, then this chapter is for you. There are walks for beginners and non-hikers as well as hikes for experienced backpackers. While this chapter centers on Great Basin National Park, it also covers hiking in the Mount Moriah Wilderness in the North Snake Range.

Backcountry Guidelines

Permits and Registration

Although permits are not currently required for day hiking or backpacking within the park, it's a good idea to check with the park rangers at either visitor center for current trail and backcountry conditions, or you can call 775-234-7331 x 7510. The park encourages backpackers to register for safety reasons.

Access and Seasons

The Wheeler Peak and Lexington Arch Day Use Areas and all ancient bristlecone pine groves are closed to camping. June through September is the primary hiking season in the park and Mount Moriah Wilderness because snow lingers at the high elevations of most of the trails. The Wheeler Peak Scenic Drive is not plowed and may not open until mid-June. Unimproved roads may be muddy and impassable until late spring.

On the Trail

Stay on trails whenever possible. The alpine environment is fragile and easily damaged. When hiking cross-country, stay on rock, sand, or gravel surfaces. Off-trail travel in the park and Mount Wilderness requires map, compass, and GPS skills to find faint trails and follow ridges, drainages, and other natural features.

Pets

Pets are not allowed on trails in Great Basin National Park, with the exception of the Lexington Arch Trail, where leashed pets are allowed. Leashed pets are allowed on trails in the Humboldt-Toiyabe National Forest and Bureau of Land Management Lands, including the Mount Moriah Wilderness.

Bicycles

Bicycles and mechanized equipment are prohibited on all trails in the park and also in the Mount Moriah Wilderness.

Hiking the Alpine Lakes Trail

Firearms

Firearms are allowed under certain conditions in the park. See the park's Firearms Regulations, www.nps.gov/grba/parkmgmt/firearms-regulations.htm, for more information. Hunting is not allowed in Great Basin National Park; it is allowed, subject to Nevada hunting regulations, in the Mount Moriah Wilderness, the Humboldt-Toiyabe National Forest, and on Bureau of Land Management lands.

Smoking

Smoking while traveling is illegal in the park and on the national forest. Smokers must stop and remain in one location until they have extinguished all smoking materials. All smoking materials must be packed out. During periods of high fire danger, smoking may be prohibited.

Water

Day hikers should carry all the water they need. Backpackers should carry enough water to reach an alternate water source if a planned source is dry. In the Snake Range, water is most abundant in the spring after snowmelt. By late summer, many springs and stream may be dry. All water must be purified before use to remove harmful organisms, which can be present in any water source. Stay hydrated! In this dry climate, your body often loses water insensibly, without sweating. Drink more water than is required to satisfy your thirst.

Human Waste Disposal

If facilities are available, use them. In the backcountry, human waste must be disposed of at least 100 feet from any trail or water source. Human waste should be buried in a "cat-hole" 4 to 6 inches deep. Toilet paper must be packed out and disposed of in restroom facilities.

Camping

Backcountry camping is not permitted within 0.25 mile of roads, buildings, or campgrounds, or within the Wheeler Peak and Lexington Arch Day Use areas, or within any ancient bristlecone pine grove. Camping is prohibited at all parking areas, trailheads, and along all other roads, except for the designated primitive campsites along the Strawberry Creek and Snake Creek roads.

Campsites must be a minimum of 100 feet from a stream, spring, lake or other natural body of water and at least 500 feet from any obvious archaeological site, such as mines, cabins, rock shelters, and pictograph sites. Camp on mineral soil if possible, and avoid camping above timberline. The stay limit at any campsite is 14 days.

Group Size

Groups are limited to 15 persons and/or six pack animals in the backcountry. Larger groups must split into smaller groups to meet these limits and must camp at least

Camping is not allowed within 100 feet of water sources or within the Lexington Arch and Wheeler Peak Day Use areas

0.5-mile apart. Within the park, larger groups may request an exception to these limits in the form of a Special Use Permit.

Fires

Campfires are not allowed above 10,000 feet. Backcountry users may only use liquid-or gas-fueled stoves above 10,000 feet, and are strongly encouraged to use them everywhere. Baker and Johnson Lake are above 10,000 feet and campfires are prohibited at both lakes.

Below 10,000 feet, only dead and down wood may be collected. Bristlecone pine wood may not be burned, even if dead and down. Bristlecone wood lasts for centuries and can be tree-ring dated by researchers for studies of past climate. During periods of high fire danger all fires may be prohibited, including smoking and charcoal.

Fires may only be built in areas of of bare mineral soil at least 10 feet in diameter, or in a shallow snow pit. Vegetation must be naturally clear of this 10-foot circle to prevent escape of the fire. Metal fire pans or blankets may also be used for additional protection. Clearing of vegetation is prohibited for any reason. Construction of rock fire rings is prohibited. Fires must not exceed two feet in diameter and must be attended at all times.

Before leaving, all fires must be completely extinguished by dousing with water and mixing until the ashes are cold to the touch. Burying a campfire under dirt does NOT put it out. All ashes must be widely scattered.

Pack Animals

Pack animals, including horses, mules, burros, and llamas are allowed on certain trails in the park and in the national forest. Scatter manure piles at trailheads and campsites. Picket, hobble, or graze animals at least 100 feet from any water source. All packed feed must be certified weed-free. For more information, see the Horseback Riding chapter.

Hazards

All backcountry users must be experienced, equipped, and prepared for wilderness hazards, including hypothermia, dehydration, altitude sickness, and sun exposure.

Abandoned mines are common and can be unstable and extremely dangerous. Never enter any shaft or tunnel.

Weather

Elevations in the Snake Range vary from 6,200 to 13,063 feet. Weather conditions are variable and can change rapidly. Above timberline, life-threatening thunderstorms, lightning, high wind, and snow storms can occur any time of the year. Dress in layers and bring extra clothing.

Downed bristlecone pine on The Table, Mount Moriah Wilderness

Using the Hike Descriptions

Many of the trails in the park and the Mount Moriah Wilderness are not maintained, faint, obscured by cattle trails, or confused by old jeep tracks. Except on the Wheeler Peak, Alpine Lakes, Bristlecone-Glacier, Baker Lake, and Lexington Arch Trails, hikers should carry the USGS topographic maps of the hike, and be familiar with map reading and land navigation.

Each hike description contains the following information:

Hike number and name: The hike number is also shown on the hike location map.

Distance and type of hike: This section lists the total distance of the hike in miles, including the return for out-and-back hikes. Out-and-back hikes use the same route for the return. Shuttle hikes are one-way hikes requiring a second vehicle left at the end of the hike and the distance given is one-way. Loop hikes return to the starting point and the distance is the length of the loop. All hikes are day hikes, unless noted as backpack trips. Distances were carefully measured with digital topographic maps for consistency but may not agree with official mileages and signs.

Time: This is the approximate time required in hours for day hikes and days for backpack trips.

Difficulty: All the hikes are rated as easy, moderate, or strenuous. This is a subjective rating, but in general, easy hikes can be done by nearly anyone and take a few hours at most. Moderate hikes take all or most of a day and require moderate physical abilities. Strenuous hikes are long with significant elevation change, requiring a full day or several days to accomplish. These hikes should be attempted only by experienced hikers in good physical condition.

Elevation or elevation change: If the trail is level, this gives the trail elevation. For trails that are not level, this line lists the total altitude change in feet. Elevation change does not include minor ups-and-downs along trails and routes.

Season: The best time of year to do the hike.

Permits: Whether or not permits are required

Water: A listing of springs, creeks, and lakes along the trail, primarily for backpackers but also for emergency use by dayhikers. Remember that any water source can dry up. All backcountry water should be purified.

Maps: The USGS 7.5-minute topographic maps covering the hike.

Finding the trailhead: Driving directions from the town of Baker to the trailhead, in miles. GPS coordinates are also listed, in Universal Transverse Mercator coordinates (UTM) based on the WGS84 datum.

Key Points: Except for very short trails and nature trails, this section lists key points along the hike, such as trail junctions and important landmarks. Where useful, GPS coordinates are given in UTM, using the WGS84 datum. Distances in miles are given from the start of the hike.

Hike description: The detailed description of the hike, along with interesting natural and human history. The description uses references to landmarks rather than distances wherever possible.

Recommended Hikes

Easy Day Hikes

2 Strawberry Creek, 7 Alpine Lakes

Early Season

1 Osceola Tunnel, 3 Osceola Ditch Interpretive Trail, 9 Mountain View Nature Trail, 12 Pole Canyon, 13 Can Young Canyon

Hikes for Families

1 Osceola Tunnel, 3 Osceola Ditch Interpretive Trail, 7 Alpine Lakes, 9 Mountain View Nature Trail, 17 Snake Creek

First Night in the Wilderness

12 Pole Canyon

Long Day Hikes

4 Lehman Creek Trail, 8 Bristlecone-Glacier Trail, 10 Baker and Johnson Lakes, 11 Timber Creek, 14 Johnson Lake, 17 South Fork Big Wash, 21 The Table

Hikes for Photographers

5 Bald Mountain, 6 Wheeler Peak, 7 Alpine Lakes, 8 Bristlecone-Glacier Trail, 14 Johnson Lake, 18 Lexington Arch, 21 The Table

Hikes With Lots of Side Trips and Exploring

11 Baker and Johnson Lakes, 11 Timber Creek-South Fork Baker Creek, 14 Johnson Lake, 19 Smith Creek, 20 Hendrys Creek, 21 The Table

Hikes for Peak Baggers

5 Bald Mountain, 6 Wheeler Peak, 20 Hendrys Creek, 21 The Table

Hikes for Backpackers

10 Baker and Johnson Lakes, 11 Timber Creek, 14 Johnson Lake, 15 Dead Lake, 17 South Fork Big Wash, 20 Hendrys Creek, 21 The Table

Hiking in Great Basin National Park

These hikes are in the South Snake Range, in and around Great Basin National Park. Dogs are not allowed on trails in the park, with the exception of Lexington Arch Trail, where pets are allowed on leashes no longer than six feet. Horses and pack animals are allowed on all trails except: Wheeler Peak Day Use Area trails, Osceola Ditch Trail, Lexington Arch Trail, and Baker to Johnson Lake Cutoff Trail. For the latest trail information, contact the park (see the Resources chapter.)

1 Osceola Tunnel

This is an easy walk to a historic, hand-dug tunnel which was built to support a gold mining operation.

- Distance: 1.4 miles out-and-back
- Time: 1 hour
- Difficulty: Easy
- Elevation change: 8,000 to 8,240 feet
- Season: All year
- Permits: Day hikers are requested to sign in at the trailhead, if a register is available. Backpackers are encouraged to voluntarily register at a park visitor center
- Water: None
- Maps: USGS: Windy Peak
- Finding the Trailhead: From Baker, drive 5.0 miles northwest on NV 487, then turn left on US 6-50. Go 3.3 miles, then turn left on an unsigned, paved road which goes toward a maintenance facility. At 0.3 miles, just before reaching the facility, turn right on a signed dirt road to Strawberry Creek. Continue another 5.2 miles to a "Road Closed" sign on the right, next to a lone tree. This unsigned trailhead is in the middle of the meadow at the head of Strawberry Creek. UTM: Zone 11 733074mE 4326333mN

Key Points

- 0.0 Unsigned trailhead at the "Road Closed" sign (UTM: Zone 11 733074mE 4326333mN)
- 0.7 Osceola Tunnel (UTM: Zone 11 732413mE 4326848mN)- return the way you came
- 1.4 Unsigned trailhead.

The Hike

The trail follows the old, closed jeep track across the meadow and up the hillside to the pass visible to the northwest. This is an easy, enjoyable walk with nice views of upper Strawberry Valley and the beautiful, forested slopes of Bald Mountain. When you reach the pass, go through the gate (please leave it as you found it) and walk down the road a short distance to the north. Look for mine tailings below to the left, then drop down the short slope. This is the exit point for a tunnel dug through the rock under the pass you just walked over. This allowed water from the Eastern Osceola Ditch to get to this point without having to contour miles around the hill to the east. Though little remains of the tunnel, the continuation of the ditch is visible several hundred feet lower on the hillsides to the northwest. Apparently the water flowed down a wooden chute for about 400 vertical feet before being collected into a ditch again. For details on the Osceola Ditch, see Hike 3.

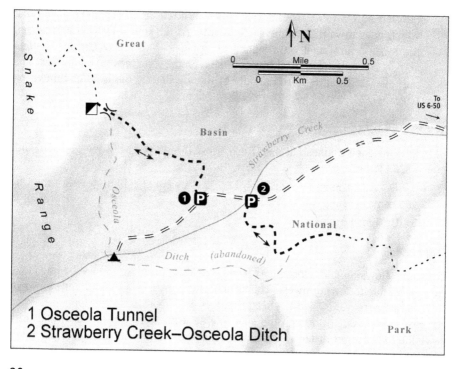

1 Osceola Tunnel
2 Strawberry Creek–Osceola Ditch

2 Strawberry Creek-Osceola Ditch

This is a very easy walk to the historic Osceola Ditch, with an option for a longer hike along the route of the old ditch.

- Distance: 1.0 mile out-and-back; longer optional
- Time: 1 hour (longer optional)
- Difficulty: Easy
- Elevation change: 7,960 to 8,200 feet
- Season: All year
- Permits: Day hikers are requested to sign in at the trailhead, if a register is available. Backpackers are encouraged to voluntarily register at a park visitor center
- Water: Strawberry Creek
- Maps: USGS: Windy Peak
- Finding the Trailhead: From Baker, drive 5.0 miles northwest on NV 487, then turn left on US 6-50. Go 3.3 miles, then turn left on an unsigned, paved road which goes toward a maintenance facility. At 0.3 miles, just before reaching the facility, turn right on a signed dirt road to Strawberry Creek. Continue 5.0 miles, then turn left instead of crossing the creek a final time. Go 0.1 mile to a primitive campsite at the end of the road, which is the trailhead for this hike. UTM: Zone 11 733345mE 4326273mN

Key Points

- 0.0 Unsigned trailhead at the primitive campsite (UTM: Zone 11 733345mE 4326273mN)
- 0.5 Osceola Ditch (UTM: Zone 11 733940mE 4326169mN; return the way you came
- 1.0 Unsigned trailhead

The Hike

From the trailhead, walk back down the road a few yards to an old, closed jeep trail which climbs the hill to the right (south.) Follow this road up the hillside, through an aspen grove, and up a switchback. At a junction, turn left (east) and follow the old road up to the abandoned Osceola Ditch. This vantage point has fine views of Strawberry Valley. You can also see the route of the Osceola Ditch at the head of the valley. This is the destination for this easy hike, but if desired you can follow the old road east along the route of the ditch for several miles. For more information on the history of the ditch, see Hike 3.

3 Osceola Ditch Interpretive Trail

An easy interpretive trail leads to the Osceola Ditch Historic Site just off the Wheeler Peak Scenic Road. Signs explain the history and purpose of the ditch.

- Distance: 0.6 miles out-and-back
- Time: 1.0 hour
- Difficulty: Easy
- Elevation: 8,400 feet
- Season: All year
- Permits: Day hikers are requested to sign in at the trailhead, if a register is available. Backpackers are encouraged to voluntarily register at a park visitor center
- Water: None
- Maps: USGS: Windy Peak
- Finding the Trailhead: From Baker, drive 5.0 miles west on NV 488. Just after passing the park boundary, turn right on the paved, signed Wheeler Peak Scenic Drive. Continue 4.6 miles to the signed Osceola Ditch interpretive site, and park on the right side of the highway. UTM: Zone 11 736571mE 4323492mN

Key Points

- 0.0 Osceola Ditch Interpretive Trail Trailhead (UTM: Zone 11 736571mE 4323492mN)
- 0.3 Osceola Ditch (UTM Zone 11 737028mE 4323625mN); return the way you came
- 0.6 Osceola Ditch Interpretive Trail Trailhead

The Hike

A sign at the trailhead briefly explains the history and purpose of the ditch. The trail follows a drainage downhill through the woods a short distance to reach the remains of the ditch, which contours along the hillside. When it was operational, the Osceola Ditch ran 18 miles along the Snake Range to deliver water from Lehman Creek on the east side of the range to the town of Osceola on the west side.

Why such a huge undertaking? In a word, gold. In 1872, prospectors discovered gold northwest of the present Great Basin National Park. Within five years, placer deposits were found and the gold mining picked up momentum. Placer mining can be done by hand with a gold pan, but for large scale mining it was more efficient to use hydraulic mining. In the hydraulic process, a jet of water is directed at a hillside to wash out the gravel and dislocate any gold which might be present. The water and gravel are then run through a series of sluices which separate out the heavier gold. The catch is that a large supply of water is required.

In 1884-5, a 16-mile ditch was built south along the west slopes of the range to capture water from several creeks and bring it to Osceola. But the amount of water from these streams was disappointing and the mines were able to operate for only about two hours a day. A second ditch was proposed which would divert water from the larger streams on the east side of the range. Though the new ditch would cross more difficult terrain and would be expensive, estimates of the amount of gold which could be recovered with more water seemed to indicate that the venture would be profitable. Work started in September 1889 and the ditch was finished in July the following year. Several hundred men with pack animals worked on the project and three sawmills ran full time to provide lumber. In places where the route traversed cliffs and steep rocky slopes, wooden flumes and chutes were constructed, totaling 11,600 feet. A 632-foot tunnel was blasted through the ridge north of Strawberry Creek. The cost was $108,223, only a few thousand more than originally estimated. At first, gold production increased, but there were problems with the new ditch. In the end, lawsuits over water rights, water theft, and leaking flumes caused the Eastern Osceola Ditch to fail to deliver as much water as anticipated. Dry years, starting in 1893, cut further into the water supply, and by 1901 the ditch was abandoned. Mining activity almost completely ceased by 1905.

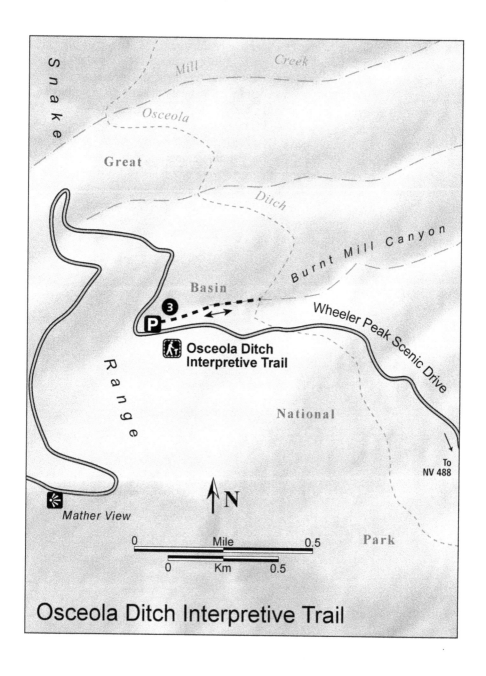

Osceola Ditch Interpretive Trail

Paintbrush in sage meadow along the Lehman Creek Trail

4 Lehman Creek Trail

This scenic hike climbs from Upper Lehman Creek Campground to Wheeler Peak Campground, skirting Lehman Creek and passing through scenic alpine meadows along the way.

- Time: 5 hours out and back, 3 hours with a shuttle
- Difficulty: Strenuous
- Elevation change: 7,750 to 9,820 feet
- Season: Summer and fall
- Permits: Day hikers are requested to sign in at the trailhead, if a register is available. Backpackers are encouraged to voluntarily register at a park visitor center. Camping is not allowed in the Wheeler Peak Day Use Area.
- Water: Upper Lehman Creek Campground, Lehman Creek, Wheeler Peak Campground
- Maps: USGS: Windy Peak
- Finding the Trailhead: From Baker, drive west 5.0 miles on NV 488, the park entrance road. Just past the park entrance, turn right (north) on the signed, paved Wheeler Peak Scenic Drive. Continue 2.4 miles to Upper Lehman Campground. Turn left at the second campground entrance, then drive to the signed trailhead. The trailhead is on the right just before the road enters the campground loop. If you have two vehicles, you can do a shuttle to make this an all downhill hike. To reach the Wheeler Peak Campground trailhead from Upper Lehman Creek Campground, continue up the scenic drive 9.6 miles to the Bristlecone parking area just before entering the Wheeler Campground. Walk east through the campground to the start of the trail. UTM: Zone 11 737799mE 4321853mN

Key Points

- 0.0 Trailhead at Upper Lehman Creek Campground (UTM: Zone 11 737799mE 4321853mN)
- 0.7 Cross Osceola Ditch (UTM Zone 11 736609mE 4321837mN)
- 1.7 Meadow with views
- 3.4 Trailhead at the lower end of Wheeler Peak Campground (UTM: Zone 11 733692mE 4321440mN); return the way you came
- 6.8 Trailhead at Upper Lehman Creek Campground (UTM: Zone 11 737799mE 4321853mN)

The Hike

The trail is well maintained and easy to follow as it climbs steadily through a mountain mahogany thicket, away from Lehman Creek. After a while the trail returns to the creek; watch for the remains of the old Osceola Ditch, which the trail crosses. You can follow the ditch to the creek, but there is no trace of the original structure used to divert the creek. After crossing the old ditch, the trail stays near the creek in a cool, dense fir and aspen forest. Then it swings away from the creek and climbs up a ridge to enter a meadow at about 9,100 feet with good views of Jeff Davis and Wheeler Peaks. The Wheeler Glacier is hidden behind a ridge. Above the meadows the trail comes near the creek briefly before finally swinging away and climbing a final slope in a wide switchback. The trailhead is at the east end of Wheeler Peak Campground. If you desire to combine this hike with the Alpine Lakes Loop or any of the other trails which start from the campground, continue uphill to the west end of the campground and the Alpine Lakes Trailhead. Otherwise, return to Upper Lehman Campground the way you came.

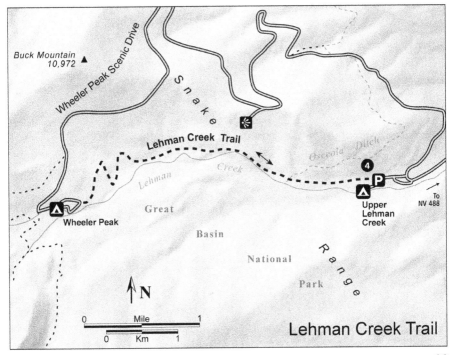

Lehman Creek Trail

Wheeler Peak from the route up Bald Mountain

5 Bald Mountain

This trail and cross-country hike leads to the rounded, gentle summit of Bald Mountain, which offers fine views of Wheeler Peak and Jeff Davis Peak. Bald Mountain is a much easier summit to reach than its higher, more famous neighbor, Wheeler Peak.

- Distance: 6.0 miles out-and-back
- Time: 5 hours
- Difficulty: Moderate
- Elevation change: 9,960 to 11,562 feet
- Season: Summer and fall
- Permits: Day hikers are requested to sign in at the trailhead, if a register is available. Backpackers are encouraged to voluntarily register at a park visitor center. Camping is not allowed in the Wheeler Peak Day Use Area.
- Water: Wheeler Peak Campground
- Maps: USGS: Windy Peak
- Finding the Trailhead: From Baker, drive about 5.0 miles west on NV 488. Just after passing the park boundary, turn right on the paved, signed Wheeler Peak Scenic Drive. Continue 12.0 miles to the signed Bristlecone Trailhead just before entering the Wheeler Campground at the end of the road. UTM: Zone 11 733103mE 4321322mN

Key Points

- 0.0 Bristlecone Trailhead (UTM: Zone 11 733103mE 4321322mN)
- 0.1 Junction with Bristlecone-Glacier Trail; turn right (UTM Zone 11 733121mE mN)
- 0.7 Junction with Summit Trail; turn left (UTM: Zone 11 732448mE 4321229mN)
- 0.8 Junction with Wheeler Peak Trail; turn right (UTM: Zone 11 732266mE 4321031mN)
- 2.0 Wheeler Saddle; go north, cross-country (UTM: Zone 11 731810mE 4320749mN)
- 3.0 Bald Mountain (UTM: Zone 11 731783mE 4322404mN); return the way you came
- 6.0 Bristlecone Trailhead (UTM: Zone 11 733103mE 4321322mN)

The Hike

Start from the trailhead parking at Wheeler Peak Campground by walking across the road to the Alpine Lakes Trailhead. The trail crosses Lehman Creek on a foot bridge and climbs gradually through the dense forest. Turn right at the junction with the Bristlecone-Glacier Trail. The trail crosses the creek again and enters a series of alpine meadows. At the signed junction with the Summit Trail turn left. After a short distance, turn right on the Wheeler Peak Trail. Stay on this trail until it reaches Wheeler Saddle, almost directly above Stella Lake. Now turn right (north) and walk cross-country up the easy ridge. Here, right at timberline, stunted Engelmann spruce and bristlecone pine are the last outposts of the forest. Some of the trees have formed classic krummholz, a term that refers to the low matted forms that timberline trees tend to take. In winter, snow covers the krummholz, insulating the tree's foliage from the bitter wind and driven snow.

Our route continues right up the broad ridge as it climbs gently to the rounded summit of Bald Mountain at 11,562 feet. The view takes in the north slopes of the South Snake Range, the Mount Moriah massif in the North Snake Range, and the plunging cliffs on Wheeler and Jeff Davis Peaks.

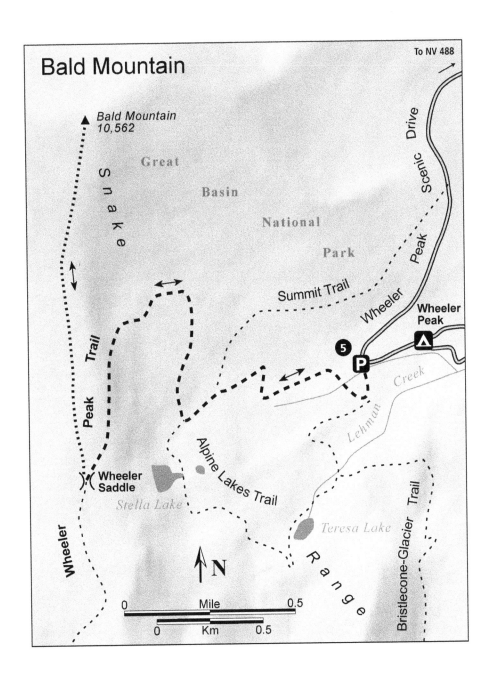

Wheeler Peak

6 Wheeler Peak

This trail leads to the top of Wheeler Peak, the highest summit in the Snake Range and second highest in Nevada. Attractions include a panoramic view of the Snake Range and the surrounding deserts 7,000 feet below, and an historic site associated with the early exploration of the West.

- Distance: 8.0 miles out-and-back
- Time: 7 hours
- Difficulty: Strenuous
- Elevation change: 10,160 to 13,063 feet
- Season: Summer through fall
- Permits: Day hikers are requested to sign in at the trailhead, if a register is available. Backpackers are encouraged to voluntarily register at a park visitor center. Camping is not allowed in the Wheeler Peak Day Use Area.
- Water: Wheeler Peak Campground
- Maps: USGS: Wheeler Peak, Windy Peak
- Finding the Trailhead: From Baker, drive west 5.0 miles on the Great Basin National Park entrance road (NV 488), then turn right (north) on the Wheeler Peak Scenic Drive. Continue 11.5 miles to the signed Summit Trailhead (this trailhead is about 0.5 miles from the end of the road.) UTM: Zone 11 733488mE 4322167mN

Key Points

- 0.0 Summit Trailhead (UTM: Zone 11 733488mE 4322167mN)
- 1.0 Junction with the Alpine Lakes Trail; turn right (UTM: Zone 11 732448mE 4321229mN)
- 1.2 Junction with Wheeler Peak Trail; turn right (UTM: Zone 11 732266mE 4321031mN)
- 2.2 Pass through Wheeler Saddle (UTM: Zone 11 731810mE 4320749mN)
- 4.0 Wheeler Peak (UTM: Zone 11 732661mE 4318632mN); return the way you came
- 8.0 Summit Trailhead (UTM: Zone 11 733488mE 4322167mN)

The Hike

Follow the Summit Trail as it climbs gradually southwest through stands of aspen along the southern slopes of Bald Mountain. Openings in the forest provide outstanding views of Wheeler and Jeff Davis Peaks. The Alpine Lakes Trail joins from the left; continue a short distance west then turn sharply right on the signed Wheeler Peak Trail.

The trail ascends the southeast slopes of Bald Mountain through a broad meadow with some fine views of the big peaks to the north. Before long the trail switches back to the south; please do not cut the switchback as the alpine vegetation is very fragile. Continue along the slope until you gain the ridge crest. Stunted and gnarled limber pine and Engelmann spruce, the last vestiges of forest, struggle to survive at treeline. Views are commanding both to the east and west. The clear, shallow waters of Stella Lake are visible, well below to the east. Above this point, the trail is above timberline and exposed to the high altitude weather; be certain the weather is good and that you have warm clothing, and especially a wind breaker, before you continue.

Follow the trail as it climbs south up the broad north ridge of Wheeler Peak. The ridge narrows, and there is a short respite from the climb at about 11,800 feet. The trail becomes steeper as it begins the final ascent. Views down the west slopes are stunning; the entire 7,000 foot sweep of the west ridge is visible from the summit to the floor of Spring Valley. Use care in this section if parts of the trail are snow covered. In early season, large snowfields may block parts of the trail. These snowfields may be very dangerous, as the snow is slippery and ends above high cliffs to the north. If necessary to avoid snow, deviate to the right (south) of the trail.

Surprisingly, there are small patches of alpine plants and flowers growing in sheltered areas all along the ascent, even at the summit, which is 2,000 feet above timberline. Plants growing above treeline must adapt to the arctic environment of strong wind and severe cold.

A number of rock shelters have been built by hikers for protection from the wind. Along the summit ridge to the east, you'll spot several platforms. Look carefully and you'll see that the construction was more than casual. These were tent platforms built by the Wheeler Survey, which occupied the summit during the summer and fall for four years starting in 1881. The purpose was to precisely measure the distance and direction to other mountain peaks. This work, coordinated with other federal surveys, resulted in the first accurate network of surveyed points spanning the continent.

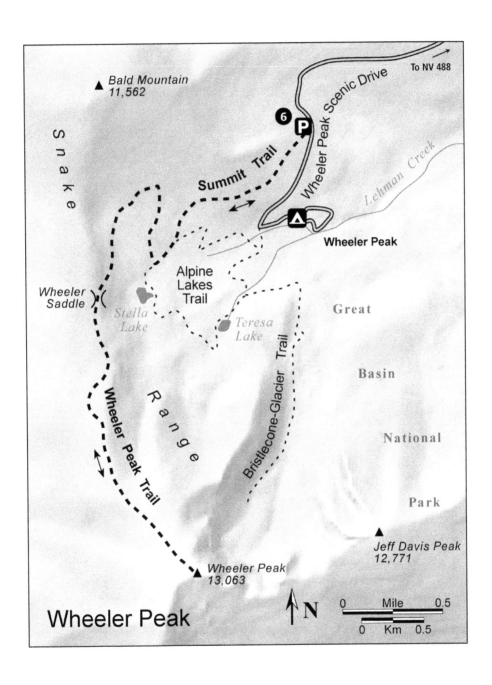

Wheeler Peak

Stella Lake

7 Alpine Lakes

This loop hike features two unique alpine lakes and close-up views of the high peaks in the South Snake Range. The trail is well-maintained and marked, and the hike is well-suited for families and those desiring an easy and scenic walk.

- Distance: 2.7-mile loop
- Time: 1.5 hours
- Difficulty: Moderate
- Elevation change: 10,000 to 10,400 feet
- Season: Summer and fall
- Permits: Day hikers are requested to sign in at the trailhead, if a register is available. Backpackers are encouraged to voluntarily register at a park visitor center. Camping is not allowed in the Wheeler Peak Day Use Area.
- Water: Wheeler Peak Campground, Stella Lake, Teresa Lake
- Maps: USGS: Windy Peak
- Finding the Trailhead: From Baker, drive about 5.0 miles west on NV 488. Just after passing the park boundary, turn right on the paved, signed Wheeler Peak Scenic Drive. Continue 12.0 miles to the signed Bristlecone Trailhead just before entering the Wheeler Campground at the end of the road. UTM: Zone 11 733103mE 4321322mN

Key Points

- 0.0 Bristlecone Trailhead (UTM: Zone 11 733103mE 4321322mN)
- 0.1 After crossing the bridge across Lehman Creek, stay right on the Alpine Lakes Trail
- 0.2 Bristlecone-Glacier Trail; turn right (UTM: Zone 11 733121mE 4321166mN)
- 0.7 Junction with Summit Trail; turn left (UTM: Zone 11 732448mE 4321229mN)
- 0.8 Junction with Wheeler Peak Trail; stay left (UTM: Zone 11 732266mE 4321031mN)
- 1.0 Stella Lake (UTM: Zone 11 732201mE 4320861mN)
- 1.8 Teresa Lake (UTM: Zone 11 732774mE 4320535mN)
- 2.1 Bristlecone-Glacier Trail; stay left (UTM: Zone 11 733007mE 4320792mN)
- 2.5 Alpine Lakes Trail; stay right (UTM: Zone 11 733121mE 4321166mN)
- 2.6 Stay left on the Bristlecone-Glacier Trail
- 2.7 Bristlecone Trailhead (UTM: Zone 11 733103mE 4321322mN)

The Hike

Although the Alpine Lakes Trail is relatively short with little elevation gain, it lies at 10,000 feet. Most people, especially those who live at sea level, will have less hiking ability at this elevation. The trail crosses Lehman Creek on a small foot bridge, then forks after a short distance. Turn right on the Alpine Lakes Trail, which climbs through Engelmann spruce-limber pine forest to the north of the creek. After crossing the creek again, the pleasant trail switchbacks to the right through meadows bordered with quaking aspen. There are fine views of Wheeler Peak. Stay left at the junction with the Summit Trail. A short distance farther, the Wheeler Peak Trail turns sharply right; continue straight ahead to the first lake.

Stella Lake is a typical glacial lake formed in the cirque created by a glacier. The moving ice "grinds down at the heel" and forms a depression in the floor of the steep-walled valley at its head. After the ice melts, a deep cold lake is often left behind. Erosion of the steep mountainsides above the lake gradually fills it in. Stella Lake is in the last stages of fill; it is shallow and freezes almost solid in the winter.

The trail skirts Stella Lake on the left then wanders through uneven, hummocky terrain. A glacier once covered this area; when it melted, it dropped its mixed load of dirt, sand, rocks and boulders in a jumbled heap. Sometimes large blocks of ice are left behind and isolated from the retreating mass of the main glacier and later melt to form kettle lakes in depressions in the moraine. There are a number of depressions along this section of the trail that could contain small lakes, but don't. This is probably because of the drier climate at present.

The trail now descends in a single switchback and follows a small stream to Teresa Lake. The depth of this lake varies greatly, depending on the amount of snow melt. The trail skirts the lake on the left then continues down the drainage. Just north of the lake, turn left at a junction with the Bristlecone-Glacier Trail. (This trail can be done as a side trip; it adds 3.2 miles to the length. See the Bristlecone-Glacier Trail for details.) The trail continues north down the slope, and soon reaches the junction with the Alpine Lakes Trail where we started the loop. Stay right to reach the trailhead.

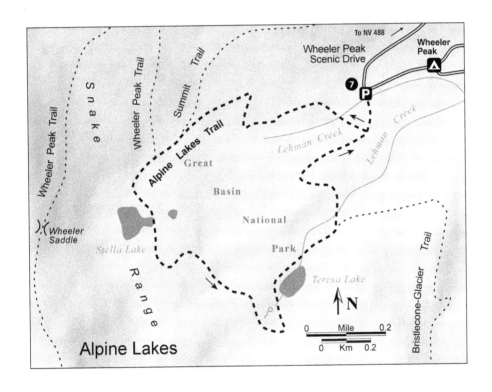

Alpine Lakes

Wheeler Glacier, the only permanent icefield between the Sierra Nevada and the Rocky Mountains

Bristlecone pine on the interpretive loop

8 Bristlecone–Glacier Trail

This trail leads to the foot of the Wheeler Glacier, which is the only permanent body of ice between the Sierra Nevada and the Wasatch Mountains. A short interpretive trail winds through a bristlecone pine grove where signs explain the natural history of the oldest living trees on earth.

- Distance: 4.6 miles out-and-back
- Time: 3 hours
- Difficulty: Moderate
- Elevation change: 9,800 to 10,900 feet
- Season: Summer and fall
- Permits: Day hikers are requested to sign in at the trailhead, if a register is available. Backpackers are encouraged to voluntarily register at a park visitor center. Camping is not allowed in the Wheeler Peak Day Use Area.
- Water: Wheeler Peak Campground, Teresa Lake
- Maps: USGS: Windy Peak
- Finding the Trailhead: From Baker, drive about 5.0 miles west on NV 488. Just after passing the park boundary, turn right on the paved, signed Wheeler Peak Scenic Drive. Continue 12.0 miles to the signed Bristlecone Trailhead just before entering the Wheeler Campground at the end of the road. UTM: Zone 11 733103mE 4321322mN

Key Points

- 0.0 Bristlecone Trailhead (UTM: Zone 11 733103mE 4321322mN)
- 0.1 After the bridge, stay right on the Bristlecone-Glacier Trail
- 0.2 Bristlecone-Glacier Trail; go left (UTM: Zone 11 733121mE 4321166mN)
- 0.6 Alpine Lakes Trail; go left (UTM: Zone 11 733007mE 4320792mN)
- 1.7 Bristlecone interpretive loop (UTM: Zone 11 733404mE 4320196mN)
- 2.3 Glacier viewpoint; return the way you came (UTM: Zone 11 733058mE 4319184mN)
- 4.6 Bristlecone Trailhead (UTM: Zone 11 733103mE 4321322mN)

The Hike

The trail crosses Lehman Creek on a footbridge; stay right on the Bristlecone-Glacier Trail. then reaches a signed trail junction. Here, turn left on the signed Bristlecone-Glacier Trail. This trail climbs steadily through dense limber pine-Engelmann spruce forest, then meets the Alpine Lakes Trail at a signed junction. (Teresa Lake is a short distance up the Alpine Lakes Trail.) Turn left (east) and follow the Bristlecone-Glacier Trail as it first crosses over a low ridge, then climbs across a shady north-facing slope. Where the trail turns right around the ridge, there is a good view of the upper Lehman Creek drainage and the Wheeler Peak Campground. Now the trail starts climbing gently along the slope. A switchback leads onto the rough, jumbled terrain of the moraine left by the retreat of the

Wheeler Glacier. There is a short, signed interpretive trail here which explains the bristlecone pines. It is certainly worth the time and adds almost nothing to the hike distance.

The bristlecone pine is a gnarled, tough tree found near timberline in the mountains of the Intermountain West. It is easily recognized by its short, stiff needles growing five to a bundle; the branches resemble neat bottle brushes. The species of bristlecone pine found in Nevada and eastern California lives more than 4,500 years and are among the oldest living things on earth.

Researchers determine the ages of the trees using tree ring dating. A slender cylinder is screwed into the heart of the tree in a process which leaves the tree unharmed. The cylinder is removed and the wood core extracted. Bands along the core are sections of the tree rings, and each ring represents a period of growth. Since bristlecones have one short period of growth each year, the rings may be counted and correlated with other tree ring data to accurately determine the tree's age, as well as indicate climate changes affecting the tree's growth rate. By correlating overlapping sections from older, and dead trees, the tree ring record has been extended back 9,000 years.

The two trails rejoin at a signed junction, and the Bristlecone-Glacier Trail continues up the moraine. The only trees that survive now are low mats of bristlecone pine, limber pine and Engelmann spruce. The trail ends at the foot of the Wheeler rock glacier. In this stark canyon carved by ice and frost, life is reduced to a few hardy tundra plants growing in places where the rocks are stable. But even on the snow of the glacier there is life. In late summer you may notice a red stain on the old snow. This is caused by an alga which lives on snowfields.

Glaciers form when the annual snowfall exceeds that lost to melting and evaporation. As the layers of snow pile up year after year, their weight compresses the lowest layers into ice. Under such great pressure, ice becomes fluid and begins to flow down the mountainside. The moving ice scours its bed, wearing away the bedrock and moving it downhill. The lower end of the glacier is at the elevation where the ice melts faster than it is replaced. Even a slight change in the climate can cause a rapid retreat or expansion of a glacier, so scientists study glaciers worldwide as a sensitive indicator of climate change. When a glacier retreats, it drops its immense load of rock into an unsorted heap of dirt, gravel, and rocks of all sizes- a "moraine."

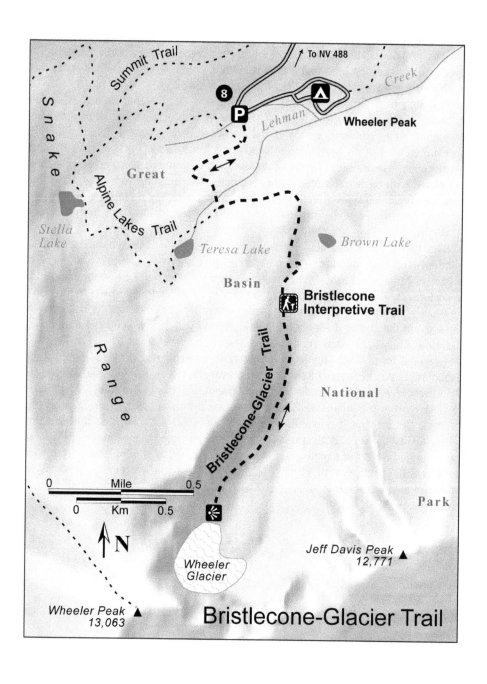

9 Mountain View Nature Trail

An interpretive trail that explains the natural history of the surrounding pinyon-juniper plant community as well the geology of the Snake Range, this nature trail is a great walk for families with small children.

- Distance: 0.3 mile loop
- Time: 0.5 hour
- Difficulty: Easy
- Elevation: 6,820 feet
- Season: All year
- Permits: None
- Water: Visitor center
- Maps: A guide leaflet is available at the visitor center
- Finding the Trailhead: From Baker, drive west on NV 488 and park at the park Visitor Center. UTM: Zone 11 740742mE 4321089mN

The Hike

The nature trail is a good way to become familiar with the pinyon-juniper plant community. It starts at the north end of the visitor center at the old Rhodes Cabin. The cabin was a guest lodge during the early days of Lehman Caves National Monument. The trail continues behind the cabin, gradually climbing the slope until a viewpoint is reached. Interpretive signs along the trail point out typical plants common in the Great Basin.

Old cabin on the Baker Creek Trail

10 Baker and Johnson Lakes

This is an especially scenic loop hike that follows a cascading alpine creek to a pair of classic alpine lakes. It also crosses two high passes and traverses alpine meadows with open views of the surrounding summits. You'll also pass by the site of an historic tungsten mine.

- Distance: 13.1-mile loop; long dayhike or overnight backpack trip
- Time: 10 hours or two days
- Difficulty: Strenuous
- Elevation change: 8,000 to 11,300 feet
- Season: Summer and fall
- Permits: Day hikers are requested to sign in at the trailhead, if a register is available. Backpackers are encouraged to voluntarily register at a park visitor center
- Water: Baker Creek, Baker Lake, Johnson Lake, South Fork Baker Creek
- Maps: USGS: Wheeler Peak, Kious Spring
- Finding the Trailhead: From Baker, drive west 5.2 miles on NV 488, the entrance road to the park. Just after passing the park boundary sign, turn left (south) on the signed, maintained dirt Baker Creek Road. Follow this road 4.0 miles to its end at the signed Baker Trailhead. UTM: Zone 11 738613mE 4317778mN

Key Points

- 0.0 Baker Trailhead (UTM: Zone 11 738613mE 4317778mN)
- 4.1 Old cabin
- 4.3 Junction with Baker-Johnson Trail (UTM: Zone 11 733218mE 4315507mN)
- 5.3 Baker Lake
- 5.5 Cross-country route to Baker-Johnson Trail (UTM: Zone 11 733495mE 4315351mN)
- 5.9 Baker-Johnson Trail; turn right (UTM: Zone 11 733670mE 4315027mN)
- 6.4 Baker-Johnson pass
- 7.1 Johnson Lake
- 8.7 Junction with trail to Snake-Baker Pass; turn left (UTM: Zone 11 736238mE 4313917mN)
- 9.4 Snake-Baker Pass
- 10.0 Junction with S. Fork Baker Creek Trail; turn left (UTM: Zone 11 737430mE 4315131mN)
- 12.8 Junction with Timber Creek Trail; turn left (UTM: Zone 11 738567mE 4317592mN)
- 13.1 Baker Trailhead (UTM: Zone 11 738613mE 4317778mN)

The Hike

Start on the Baker Lake Trail. The trail climbs along the north side of boisterous Baker Creek, sometimes swinging to the north in a series of switchbacks. There are varied views of the canyon walls and the high country, especially when the trail temporarily leaves the creek and its dense riparian vegetation. Other sections of the trail stay near the creek in fine aspen groves. After a long climb, the trail passes the ruins of an old cabin. It was probably used by Peter Deishman, a prospector who was active in the early part of the century. Continue on the main trail which climbs the steep slope below Baker Lake in a series of switchbacks. Watch for a faint, unsigned trail going left to Baker-Johnson pass, but stay right on the main trail and continue to Baker Lake. This small, scenic alpine lake is backdropped by the rugged cliffs of the Snake Range crest and Baker Peak.

After enjoying the lake, start back down the trail and watch for a cairned cross-country route going right (southeast) before the main trail starts its steep descent. Follow the cairns as they contour southeast a short distance to join the faint Baker-Johnson trail in the open valley above timberline. If you don't find the trail along the creek, just follow the drainage and the cairns uphill. The route finally reaches the broad Johnson Pass at 11,294 feet. There are sweeping views, including Baker Peak, Jeff Davis Peak, and close at hand, Pyramid Peak.

Look for a few cairn, and follow them south from the pass. The trail becomes well defined on the steep slope below the pass. Early season hikers will have to avoid one or more steep snowfields. If the trail is lost under snow, pick it up farther down the slope. It soon joins a much better but still little-used trail which goes right (southwest) to the old Johnson tungsten mine, established by Alfred Johnson in the fall of 1909.

Turn left, downhill, and continue to the south shore of Johnson Lake. You'll pass more relics of the old mine, including an aerial tram cable spanning the talus slope up to the mine. Timbers and other old mining gear are scattered along the east shore of the lake, apparently brought down by a major snow avalanche in 1935. This event destroyed most of the mine workings and put an end to an already marginal venture.

The trail, now an old jeep road, continues down the drainage east of the lake and gradually becomes more distinct. Watch for the ruins of several old cabins used by the mining operation. There are numerous good camping spots in this area, and water is available in the creek. The trail descends steeply after the cabins. About a mile below Johnson Lake, the trail passes the ruins of a large log structure, the old Johnson mill. Ore was brought down to Johnson Lake via the aerial tram, then transported on mules to the mill. After being concentrated, mules carried the tungsten ore on down the mountain and eventually to the railhead at Frisco, Utah. Transportation costs would have been high, which probably contributed to the closure of the mine.

There is more camping in the forest below the mill, on the south side of the trail, though water would have to be carried down from the creek. About 0.3 miles after the mill, you'll pass an old road closure gate; this is the signal to start watching on the left for the signed trail to the Snake-Baker pass. The foot trail is little-used and easy to miss. It climbs steadily through aspens to reach the pass, where the trail becomes faint. Turn left (north), and descend the trail to the northeast through the forest below the pass.

Shortly, the trail emerges into a broad meadow. A wide pass is visible above to the right. Follow the faint trail across the meadow toward this pass. Just as it starts to climb, a sign points out the South Fork Baker Creek Trail to the left, and Timber Creek Trail ahead, over the pass. Turn left (west) and descend the faint South Fork Baker Creek Trail down the meadow into the South Fork. (This junction is shown incorrectly on the USGS map.) You'll pick up the trail again as it nears the right side of the creek where it enters the trees. From the junction, it's about 2.6 miles to a signed junction with the Timber Creek Trail. Turn left and cross three bridges across Baker Creek to reach the Baker Trailhead.

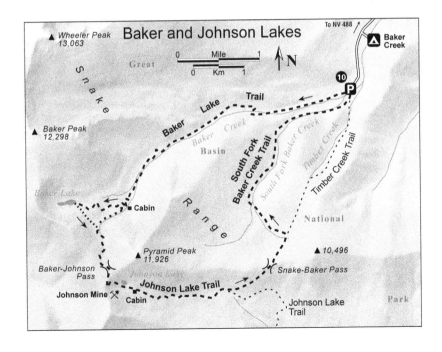

Alpine flowers above timberline

11 Timber Creek

This is a less-used trail to a high pass and scenic alpine meadows. It climbs along one alpine creek and descends alongside another and passes through high mountain forests of Engelmann spruce and quaking aspen. This hike is especially good in the fall when the aspens are changing.

- Distance: 5.3-mile loop; dayhike or overnight backpack trip
- Time: 4 hours or two days
- Difficulty: Strenuous
- Elevation change: 8,000 to 9,810 feet
- Season: Summer and fall
- Permits: Day hikers are requested to sign in at the trailhead, if a register is available. Backpackers are encouraged to voluntarily register at a park visitor center
- Water: Timber Creek, South Fork Baker Creek
- Maps: USGS: Wheeler Peak, Kious Spring
- Finding the Trailhead: From Baker, drive west 5.2 miles on NV 488, the entrance road to the park. Just after passing the park boundary sign, turn left (south) on the signed, maintained dirt Baker Creek Road. Follow this road 4.0 miles to its end at the signed Baker Trailhead. UTM: Zone 11 738613mE 4317778mN

Key Points

- 0.0 Baker Trailhead (UTM: Zone 11 738613mE 4317778mN)
- 0.1 Timber Creek Trail junction; turn left (UTM: Zone 11 738567mE 4317592mN)
- 1.8 Timber Creek pass
- 2.0 S. Fork Baker Creek Trail junction; turn right (UTM: Zone 11 737430mE 4315131mN)
- 4.6 Timber Creek Trail junction; turn left (UTM: Zone 11 738567mE 4317592mN)
- 4.7 Baker Trailhead (UTM: Zone 11 738613mE 4317778mN)

The Hike

Two trails leave the Baker Trailhead. Take the left trail, signed Johnson Lake. Cross Baker Creek on a couple of foot bridges, then watch for the signed junction with the Timber Creek Trail. Go left (south) here, and follow the sometimes faint trail as it crosses a meadow into Timber Creek Canyon. The trail begins to climb steeply and continues through a beautiful fir and aspen forest. A set of log steps marks the point where the climb starts to relent, and soon afterward the trail comes out onto a wide sage-covered saddle, framed by aspens. Cross the saddle and descend west into the head of the South Fork Baker Creek, below the striking east face of Pyramid Peak. The trail is faint across the meadow; just head down into the South Fork. The trail becomes obvious again as it enters the aspens, following the right (east) side of the creek. The South Fork trail is better maintained than the Timber Creek Trail. It's also slightly longer, so the descent is more gradual. A steeper descent in the lower part of the canyon leads to the junction with the Timber Creek Trail; turn left (northeast) here, and cross the two foot bridges back to the trailhead.

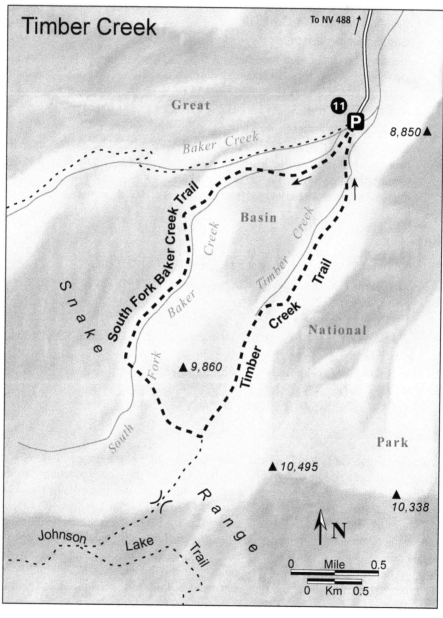

12 Pole Canyon

This hike follows a less-used, lower-elevation trail into a scenic canyon which features a permanent stream. It's a good choice when the high country is snowy or muddy.

- Distance: 4.2 miles out-and-back
- Time: 3 hours
- Difficulty: Moderate
- Elevation change: 6,820 to 7,760 feet
- Season: Spring, summer, and fall
- Permits: Day hikers are requested to sign in at the trailhead, if a register is available. Backpackers are encouraged to voluntarily register at a park visitor center
- Water: Pole Creek
- Maps: USGS: Kious Spring
- Finding the Trailhead: From Baker, drive west 5.2 miles on NV 488, the entrance road to the park. Just after passing the park boundary sign, turn left (south) on the signed, maintained dirt Baker Creek Road. Follow this road 1.6 miles, then turn left on the Gray Cliffs Road, which is also maintained dirt. Almost immediately, turn left again on an unmaintained road. Go 0.6 miles, just past a cattle guard, then park on the right at the Pole Canyon Trailhead. The trail immediately crosses Baker Creek. UTM: Zone 11 741502mE 4319419mN

Key Points

- 0.0 Pole Canyon Trailhead (UTM: Zone 11 741502mE 4319419mN)
- 2.1 Upper basin (UTM: Zone 11 739629mE 4316905mN); return the way you came
- 4.2 Pole Canyon Trailhead (UTM: Zone 11 741502mE 4319419mN)

The Hike

Due to its low elevation, this is a good hike for early season when the high country is still snow covered; it's also great in the fall when the aspens are changing. Cross Baker Creek on a footbridge. On the far side of the creek, the trail turns right and follows the left side of the creek through open pinyon-juniper country. Soon the loud rush of Baker Creek fades away, to be replaced by the gentle murmur of Pole Creek, a much smaller stream. The old road enters groves of aspen and becomes criss-crossed with deadfall. Persistence will pay off, though. Just as the deadfall is getting really annoying, the trail climbs out on the left and skirts the sage-covered slope. It passes though an aspen grove at about 7,600 feet, and emerges into the upper basin of Pole Canyon. The trail fades away here, though with care it could probably be followed to the spring shown on the topographic map. But this makes an excellent destination for the hike, with scenic views all around.

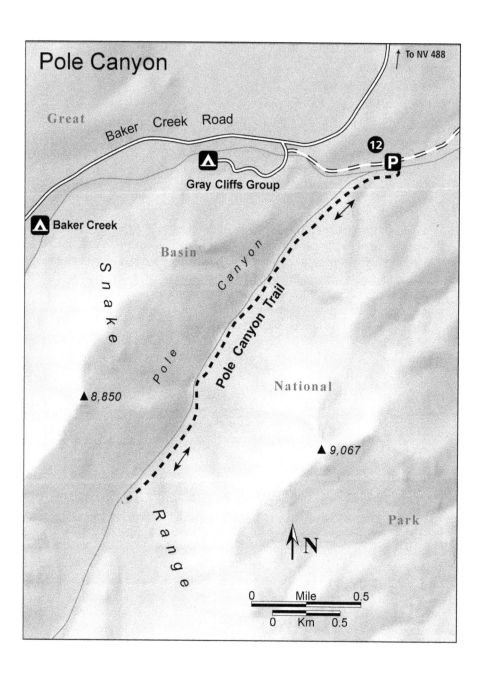

13 Can Young Canyon

This is a moderate, low elevation hike to a scenic foothills canyon which has brilliant color in the fall. It is also a good choice in the spring when higher trails in the Snake Range are still snow-packed.

- Distance: 4.8 miles out-and-back
- Time: 4 hours
- Difficulty: Moderate
- Elevation change: 6,480 to 7,200 feet
- Season: Spring, summer, and fall
- Permits: Day hikers are requested to sign in at the trailhead, if a register is available. Backpackers are encouraged to voluntarily register at a park visitor center
- Water: Can Young Canyon
- Maps: USGS: Kious Spring
- Finding the Trailhead: From Baker, drive 1.0 miles southeast on NV 487, then turn right on a maintained dirt road. The road goes past a large water tank. When 2.4 miles from the highway, turn right onto an unmaintained road, which requires a high clearance vehicle. Go right at a minor fork 2.7 miles from the highway, and continue to the park boundary at 3.5 mile. It's advisable to park here, as the road becomes much rougher ahead. UTM: Zone 11 745189mE 4317752mN

Key Points

- 0.0 Unsigned trailhead at the park boundary (UTM: Zone 11 745189mE 4317752mN)
- 0.7 Tee junction at water trough; turn right (UTM: Zone 11 744294mE 4317208mN)
- 1.1 Junction below saddle; stay left (UTM: Zone 11 744189mE 4317775mN)
- 2.1 Can Young Canyon; turn left (UTM: Zone 11 742770mE mN)
- 2.4 End of hike (UTM: Zone 11 742598mE 4317612mN); return the way you came
- 4.8 Unsigned trailhead at the park boundary (UTM: Zone 11 745189mE 4317752mN)

The Hike

From the park boundary, walk up the road. The road is seldom used and it makes a nice hike. You'll have a good view of the impressive cliffs to the left of the road. The road reaches a T intersection at a cattle watering trough in Kious Basin. Turn right, downhill, and follow the old road as it swings around another impressive cliff. A road forks right; turn left, uphill to the northwest. Within a few yards the road goes over a saddle formed by a large rock knob. Shortly after leaving the saddle, the road goes through a gate, temporarily leaving the park. After this, the road climbs slowly along the foothills, then climbs more steeply into the mouth of Can Young Canyon. Cross the flowing creek, then, at another T intersection, turn left and walk past the park boundary sign into the canyon. The road is closed to vehicles at this point. The old road continues along the creek, past fine aspen stands, before fading and becoming blocked by deadfall. This makes a good turnaround point.

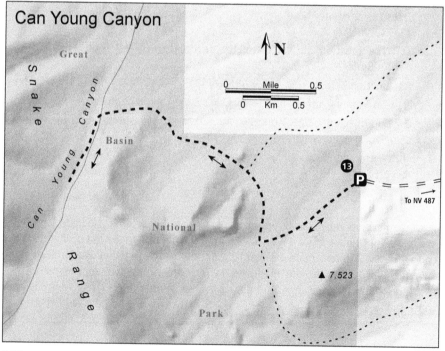

Johnson Lake

14 Johnson Lake

This is a shorter, alternate trail to Johnson Lake and the Johnson Mine historic site. The scenic trail climbs though quaking aspen groves and through cool alpine forest to the arctic-alpine tundra zone above timberline.

- Distance: 7.4 miles out-and-back; long dayhike or two day backpack trip
- Time: 6 hours or two days
- Difficulty: Strenuous
- Elevation change: 8,320 to 10,760 feet
- Season: Summer and fall
- Permits: Day hikers are requested to sign in at the trailhead, if a register is available. Backpackers are encouraged to voluntarily register at a park visitor center
- Water: Snake Creek, Johnson Lake
- Maps: USGS: Wheeler Peak
- Finding the Trailhead: From Baker, drive south 5.2 miles on NV 487, then turn right (west) on the signed, graded Snake Creek Road. Follow this road 13 miles to its end. (There are several primitive campsites along the road.) Just before the end of the road, a jeep road goes left- stay on the main road. The trailhead has a primitive campground with picnic tables, in a fine aspen grove surrounding Snake Creek. UTM: Zone 11 737958mE 4312437mN

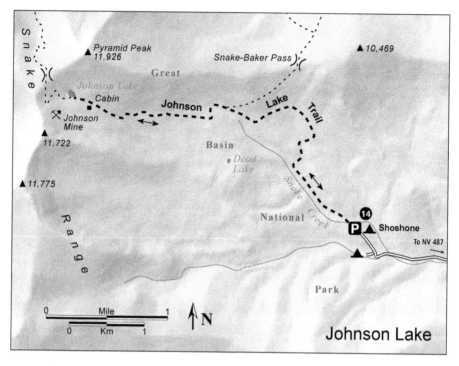

Johnson Lake

Key Points

- 0.0 Snake Creek Trailhead (UTM: Zone 11 737958mE 4312437mN)
- 2.4 Trail to Snake-Baker Pass; stay left (UTM: Zone 11 736236mE 4313903mN)
- 3.7 Johnson Lake (UTM: Zone 11 734442mE 4313850mN); return the way you came
- 7.4 Snake Creek Trailhead (UTM: Zone 11 737958mE 4312437mN)

The Hike

The Johnson Lake Trail follows an old jeep trail which is closed to vehicles. It is not marked or maintained, so you should have the topographic map. Start from the upper end of the parking lot and follow the unsigned old road directly up the hill. After a few hundred yards another jeep road comes in from the left, and the trail turns right and crosses Snake Creek. It stays north of Snake Creek all the way to Johnson Lake. After crossing the creek, the trail parallels it on the right, climbing through alpine meadows bordered with aspen and white fir.

The forest type in the Snake Range is well-represented along the Johnson Lake Trail. Great Basin trees such as curl-leaf mountain mahogany grow next to Rocky Mountain white fir and Engelmann spruce. Douglas fir is also common, as is limber pine. Along this section of the trail you should be able to identify white fir by its flat needles which will not roll in your fingers, and its spongy, cork-like bark. The needles of Douglas fir are similar but the bark is gray and more deeply furrowed.

Snake Creek

Limber pine has two inch long needles growing five to a bunch, and the limbs are very flexible, helping the tree to survive heavy alpine snow loads.

After following the creek for a while, the trail veers away to the north and descends to cross a drainage. It then climbs out onto a sage-covered slope which it ascends in a couple of switchbacks. Notice the contrast between this dry south-facing slope, covered with sage and mountain mahogany, and the moist north-facing slope you just descended, which is covered with fir and aspen.

Above the switchbacks, the trail climbs steeply through forest in which limber pine starts to appear. You will also see Engelmann spruce, whose needles grow singly like the firs, but are square in cross section so that they roll easily between your fingers. You may notice a faint trail which goes right. This trail climbs to the Snake-Baker Pass; stay left on the Johnson Lake Trail. The trail now heads a minor drainage in the forest, and climbs onto a point where the forest takes on a decidedly more alpine appearance. There are a number of campsites here but no water after the snow melts. In another half mile, the trail passes an old cabin. There are a few campsites here and there is water in the creek. Be sure to camp at least 100 feet from the water.

After the cabin the old road becomes rougher and steeper for about a half mile, then moderates a bit for the final climb to the lake. More cabins, one of them fairly elaborate, are located just below the lake. Various cut logs and rusty pieces of equipment are strewn around the cabins and the lake, indicating that a lot of activity took place here. There is even a cable strung from one of the mines high on the talus slope. Some of the cut timber might have been used to support a tramway. The lake itself is small, but the west end is deep. It is a true alpine tarn- a lake created by a glacier.

15 Dead Lake

This is a hike to a mountain stream and meadows in a seldom-visited area with the option of a longer loop hike.

- Distance: 3.4 miles out-and-back; optional 4.5-mile loop
- Time: 3 hours
- Difficulty: Moderate
- Elevation change: 8,240 to 9,600 feet
- Season: Summer and fall
- Permits: Day hikers are requested to sign in at the trailhead, if a register is available. Backpackers are encouraged to voluntarily register at a park visitor center
- Water: Snake Creek
- Maps: USGS: Wheeler Peak
- Finding the Trailhead: From Baker, drive south 5.2 miles on NV 487, then turn right (west) on the signed, graded Snake Creek Road. After 13 miles, the main road veers right, away from Snake Creek. Turn left on a faint, unmaintained road. Ignore the first left fork; take the second left fork and park at the unsigned trailhead. If you miss the turnoff, you'll reach Shoshone Primitive

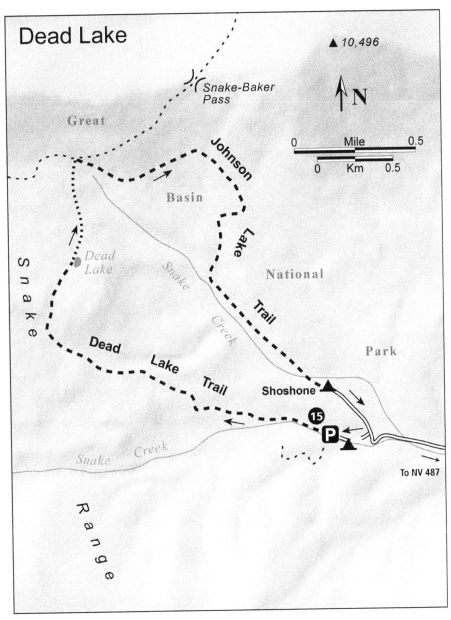

Campground at the end of the main road; backtrack the short distance to the unmaintained road. UTM: Zone 11 738008mE 4312124mN

Key Points

- 0.0 Unsigned trailhead on the unmaintained road (UTM: Zone 11 738008mE 4312124mN)

- 1.7 Dead Lake (UTM: Zone 11 736242mE 4313157mN); return the way you came unless doing the cross-country loop
- 3.4 Unsigned trailhead on the unmaintained road (UTM: Zone 11 738008mE 4312124mN)

Optional cross-country loop:

- 2.1 Walk cross-country north to the Johnson Lake Trail; turn right (UTM: Zone 11 736296mE 4313870mN)
- 4.0 Shoshone Primitive Campground (UTM: Zone 11 737958mE 4312437mN)
- 4.3 Turn right on the unmaintained road (UTM Zone 11 738247mE 4312144mN)
- 4.5 Unsigned trailhead on the unmaintained road (UTM: Zone 11 738008mE 4312124mN)

The Hike

Walk up the old road you were just driving. Soon you pass the limit of vehicle use, and the road starts to climb steadily. Pinyon-juniper and ponderosa pine give way to fir and aspen and there are occasional views to the east. The old jeep trail swings right; watch for a foot trail which branches right. A short, steep climb on this trail leads to a flat bench where the central fork of Snake Creek flows through small alpine meadows. Dead Lake is about 300 yards farther northeast.

Those hikers with the USGS map and familiar with cross-country hiking can finish with a nice loop. From the lake, contour north cross-country through the alpine forest. After about 0.6 miles, you will meet the Johnson Lake Trail, an old jeep road. Turn right and follow the trail 2.0 miles downhill to Shoshone Primitive Campground. To return to the trailhead, walk down the main road to the faint road at Snake Creek, then turn right and walk uphill a short distance to your car.

16 Snake Creek

This is an easy day hike along a fork of Snake Creek, a permanent stream.
- Distance: 0.7-mile loop
- Time: 1 hour
- Difficulty: Easy
- Elevation change: 8,240 to 8,400 feet
- Season: Summer and fall
- Permits: Day hikers are requested to sign in at the trailhead, if a register is available. Backpackers are encouraged to voluntarily register at a park visitor center
- Water: Snake Creek
- Maps: USGS: Wheeler Peak

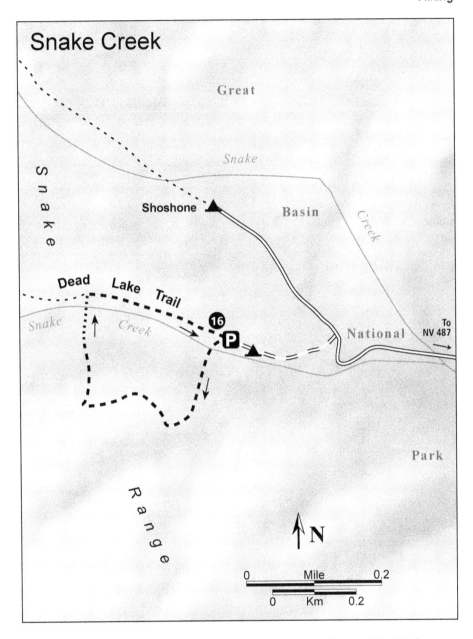

Snake Creek

• Finding the Trailhead: From Baker, drive south 5.2 miles on NV 487, then turn right (west) on the signed, graded Snake Creek Road. After 13 miles, the main road veers right, away from Snake Creek. Turn left on a faint, unmaintained road. Ignore the first left fork; take the second left fork and park at the unsigned trailhead. If you miss the turnoff, you'll reach Shoshone Primitive Campground at the end of the main road; backtrack the short distance to the unmaintained road. UTM: Zone 11 738008mE 4312124mN

Key Points

- 0.0 Unsigned trailhead at primitive campsite (UTM: Zone 11 738008mE 4312124mN)
- 0.5 End of old road (UTM: Zone 11 737643mE 4312091mN)
- 0.6 Dead Lake Trail (UTM: Zone 11 737670mE 4312238mN)
- 0.8 Unsigned trailhead at primitive campsite (UTM: Zone 11 738008mE 4312124mN)

The Hike

This short trail is worthwhile because it takes you to a tributary of Snake Creek. Cross the campground and follow the old road that climbs left (northeast) out of the camp area. Several switchbacks lead to the road's abrupt end. Now turn right and drop directly down hill, cross-country, to the creek. Cross the creek, then turn right on the Dead Lake Trail, an old road, and follow it back to the trailhead. Or just follow the creek downhill to the trailhead.

Old boiler at the sawmill site, South Fork Big Wash

17 South Fork Big Wash

This a a seldom-used trail in a remote section of the park. It passes a historic sawmill site near the head of South Fork Big Wash and then follows the canyon downstream to its confluence with the north fork.

- Distance: 10.6 miles out-and-back
- Time: 6 hours
- Difficulty: Moderate
- Elevation change: 8,400 to 6,760 feet
- Season: Summer and fall
- Permits: Day hikers are requested to sign in at the trailhead, if a register is available. Backpackers are encouraged to voluntarily register at a park visitor center
- Water: Seasonal springs at old boiler, along traverse above gorge, and at end of hike
- Maps: USGS: Arch Canyon, Kious Spring
- Finding the Trailhead: From Baker, drive southeast 10.7 miles on NV 487 (the road becomes UT 21 at the state line), then turn right on the first dirt road past Pruess Lake (signed Lexington Arch.) A high-clearance or four-wheel-drive vehicle is recommended for this road. Go west 9.6 miles, then turn right (the left fork is signed for Lexington Arch.) Continue 3.8 miles, then park at the unsigned trailhead. The trail is an old jeep road on the right (north.) UTM: Zone 11 741206mE 4304532mN

Key Points

- 0.0 Unsigned trailhead at old jeep road (UTM: Zone 11 741206mE 4304532mN)
- 0.4 Park boundary (UTM: Zone 11 740751mE 4305039mN)
- 1.3 Sawmill site in South Fork Big Wash (UTM: Zone 11 740202mE 4305555mN)
- 4.2 Trail returns to South Fork Big Wash (UTM: Zone 11 743132mE 4307322mN)
- 4.8 Park boundary (UTM: Zone 11 743901mE 4307606mN)
- 5.3 North Fork Big Wash (UTM: Zone 11 744466mE 4307960mN); return the way you came
- 10.6 Unsigned trailhead at old jeep road (UTM: Zone 11 741206mE 4304532mN)

The Hike

The old jeep road climbs steeply to a broad saddle and enters the park at a signed gate. It then descends through fir-aspen forest, switches back sharply to the right (northeast), and descends to the dry bed of South Fork Big Wash. An old steam boiler remains from an old sawmill.

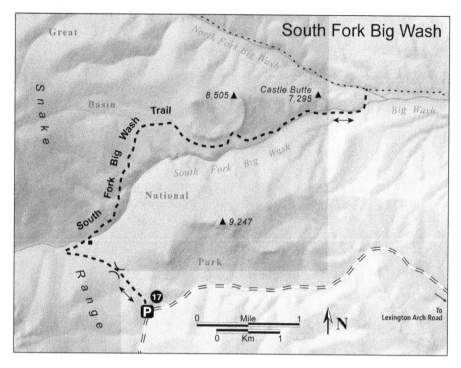

The trail continues as a foot path and climbs out on the left (north) slope. This section is faint but soon becomes more distinct. Initially, the trail goes around a juniper and crosses the flow from a spring. It climbs through dense stands of mountain mahogany, with occasional tantalizing glimpses of the narrow limestone gorge below. After leveling off, the trail passes another spring, then continues around the slope to the north. An open section of ponderosa pine and manzanita reveals a momentary view down South Fork Big Wash. After rounding a broad basin, the trail turns east and begins to descend rapidly.

It reaches the creek bed below Castle Butte, a prominent limestone cliff, then crosses to the south side. Shortly a fine spring enters from the north and puts a permanent flow in the creek. Below this point, the trail goes through a narrow slot in the limestone, made narrower still by a huge fallen boulder. This marks the approximate park boundary. The canyon opens out into a broad flat at the confluence of North Fork Big Wash, which is the end of our hike.

Lexington Arch

18 Lexington Arch

This hike follows a well-constructed trail to a unique limestone natural arch.
- Distance: 3.6 miles out-and-back
- Time: 3 hours
- Difficulty: Moderate
- Elevation change: 7,440 to 8,440 feet
- Season: Summer and fall
- Permits: Day hikers are requested to sign in at the trailhead, if a register is available. Backpackers are encouraged to voluntarily register at a park visitor center. Camping is not allowed in the Lexington Arch Day Use Area.
- Water: None
- Maps: USGS: Arch Canyon
- Finding the Trailhead: From Baker, drive southeast 10.7 miles on NV 487 (the road becomes UT 21), then turn right on the first dirt road past Pruess Lake (signed Lexington Arch.) Go west 11.7 miles, following the signs for Lexington Arch. This road is minimally maintained and a high-clearance vehicle is recommended. Due to damage from wildfire, the last mile of the road is severely washed out. Depending on your vehicle, you'll probably have to park short of the trailhead, which will add up to 2.0 miles to your hike. Please leave all gates as you find them, to help keep livestock on the correct ranges. UTM: Zone 11 743700mE 4303022mN

Key Points

- 0.0 Lexington Arch Trailhead (UTM: Zone 11 743700mE 4303022mN)
- 1.5 Lexington Arch (UTM: Zone 11 742296mE 4303169mN); return the way you came
- 3.6 Lexington Arch Trailhead (UTM: Zone 11 743700mE 4303022mN)

The Hike

At first the trail follows the drainage, but after about 200 yards it turns left and climbs the sage slope to the west in a series of broad switchbacks. It then traverses the forested south slopes of the canyon. The trail returns to the bed of the canyon at the south buttress of the arch and finally climbs into the arch itself.

Rising high above the floor of the canyon, this imposing natural arch was created by the forces of weather working slowly over a span of centuries. Lexington Arch is unusual in one important respect: it is carved from limestone. Most of the natural arches of the western United States are composed of sandstone. The fact that Lexington Arch is made of limestone leads to speculation that it was once a passage in a cave system. Flowstone, a smooth, glossy deposit that forms in caves has been found at the base of the opening, lending support to this theory.

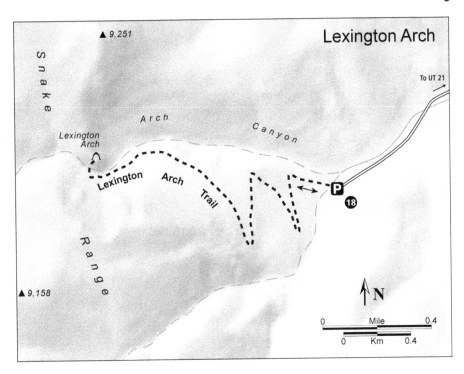

It is even possible that Lexington "Arch" is actually a natural bridge. An arch is formed by the forces of weathering, such as ice, wind, and chemical breakdown of the rock. A natural bridge, in contrast, is formed by the flowing waters of a stream. It is possible that long ago, when the canyon was less deep, the waters of Lexington Creek flowed through a cave in the wall of the canyon, in the process enlarging the tunnel that later became Lexington Arch. If this happened then the "Arch" is truly a bridge.

Hiking in Mount Moriah Wilderness

These hikes are in the North Snake Range, in and around Mount Moriah Wilderness. Dogs are allowed on these trails but must be kept under control. Horses and pack animals are allowed. Be warned, however, that most trails shown on the Forest Service and USGS maps are little-used, faint, and difficult to find. Most travel in the Mount Moriah Wilderness should be considered cross-country. For the latest trail information, contact the Humboldt-Toyaibe National Forest with the information in Resources.

19 Smith Creek

The trail takes you into a remote canyon on the north side of the Mount Moriah Wilderness which features interesting limestone caves and cliffs. It also offers potential cross-country access to The Table and the long, deep canyons draining The Table's north slopes.

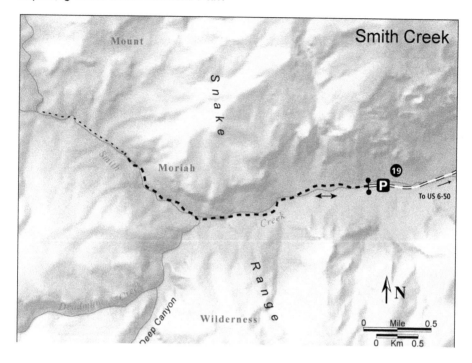

- Distance: 4.2 miles out-and-back
- Time: 4 hours
- Difficulty: Moderate
- Elevation change: 5,880 to 6,440 feet
- Season: Spring, summer, and fall
- Permits: None. Hikers should leave word of their hiking plan with a reliable person
- Water: Smith Creek
- Maps: USGS: Mount Moriah, Little Horse Canyon; USFS: Mount Moriah Wilderness
- Finding the Trailhead: From Baker, drive 5.0 miles northwest on NV 487, then turn right (east) on US 6-50, and almost immediately, take the next left (northeast.) The correct road goes past a small electrical substation. Stay on this road, which becomes maintained dirt as it heads northeast across Snake Valley, for 10.9 miles to a crossroads. Continue straight ahead on the main road to a small ranch 26.9 miles from US 6-50, then turn left on the signed Smith Creek road. Follow this non maintained dirt road 7.1 miles to its end. There are a couple of rough creek crossings near the end of the road, and their condition changes from year to year. If necessary, park and walk the last part of the road. The road is closed at the trailhead, which is the wilderness boundary. Smith Creek has water, and there's limited camping (with shade) at a small site a hundred yards before the trailhead. UTM: Zone 11 748787mE 4357884mN

Hendrys Creek

Key Points

- 0.0 Unsigned trailhead at the wilderness boundary (UTM: Zone 11 748869mE 4357876mN)
- 1.3 Deadman Creek (UTM: Zone 11 746898mE 4357449mN)
- 2.1 Trail fades out (UTM: Zone 11 745790mE 4358213mN); return the way you came
- 4.2 Unsigned trailhead at the wilderness boundary (UTM: Zone 11 748869mE 4357876mN)

The Hike

The unsigned trail up Smith Creek gets very little use. It starts as an old jeep trail and soon climbs away from the creek on the north, providing an open view of the impressive canyon. Then the trail crosses the creek and enters a cottonwood grove. Deadman Creek enters noisily from the left (south) as it pours over a series of ledges. Continue up Smith Creek on the now much fainter trail. Since it was built as a jeep road, the trail always crosses the creek when the bench peters out. The canyon becomes gradually narrower, and the high cliff on the north side is especially impressive. There are also tantalizing views of the high country, far above to the south. About 2.1 miles from the trailhead, the old trail drops into the bed of the creek and fades out. Our hike ends here, but experienced hikers can continue to Ryegrass Canyon. Other exploration possibilities are Deadman Creek and its several tributaries.

20 Hendrys Creek

The Hendrys Creek Trail gradually climbs up a scenic canyon and is an access route to The Table and Mount Moriah. A permanent stream adds to the charm of the well-maintained trail, which winds through alpine meadows graced with wildflowers.

- Distance: 19.6 miles out-and-back; long dayhike or two to three-day backpack trip
- Time: 13 hours or two days
- Difficulty: Strenuous
- Elevation change: 5,900 to 11,000 feet
- Season: Summer and fall
- Permits: None. Hikers should leave word of their hiking plan with a reliable person
- Water: Hendrys Creek
- Maps: USGS: The Cove, Old Mans Canyon, Mount Moriah; USFS: Mount Moriah Wilderness
- Finding the Trailhead: From Baker, drive 5.0 miles northwest on NV 487, then turn right (east) on US 6-50, and almost immediately, take the next left (northeast.) The correct road goes past a small electrical substation. Stay on this road, which becomes maintained dirt as it heads northeast across Snake

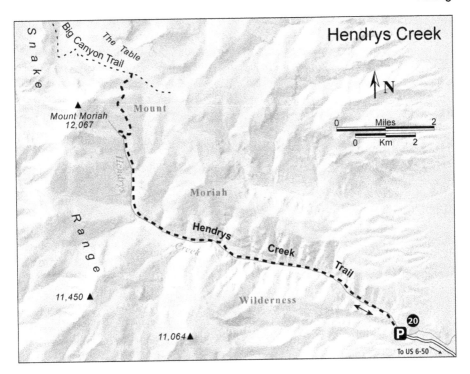

Valley, for 10.9 miles to a crossroads. Turn left (northwest) on the signed, maintained dirt road to Hendrys Creek and the Hatch Rock mining operation. Go 3.0 miles, then turn left at a sign for the trailhead; go another 0.1 miles, then turn right at an unsigned junction. After 0.3 miles, turn left at another sign for the trailhead. In another 0.6 miles, you'll pass the National Forest boundary and reach the signed trailhead. There is neither shade nor good camping at the trailhead. UTM: Zone 11 752415mE 4343810mN

Key Points

- 0.0 Hendrys Creek Trailhead (UTM: Zone 11 752415mE 4343810mN)
- 1.5 Wilderness boundary
- 5.9 Aspen meadow
- 7.5 Avalanche path
- 9.9 The Table (UTM: Zone 11 743408mE 4351865mN); return the way you came
- 19.6 Hendrys Creek Trailhead (UTM: Zone 11 752415mE 4343810mN)

The Hike

The Hendrys Creek Trail starts along the south side of the creek but soon crosses north to follow an old jeep road. The hillsides are open sage and grass, but the stream course is dense with willow and cottonwood, and a few stately ponderosa pines. Watch for occasional poison ivy along the first mile. Ponderosa pines provide some shade as the trail gradually climbs. The dramatic canyon walls, covered with pinyon pine and juniper, start to close in. You'll pass the signed wilderness boundary at about 1.5 miles. The creek runs nicely throughout, and this lower section of the canyon has plenty of camping for those who only want to walk a mile or two. After about 2.0 miles aspen start to appear, and the canyon walls become more forested.

Hendrys Creek has been a popular place for many years, as the multitude of historic inscriptions on the aspen show. At about 9,000 feet, and 5.9 miles, the trail enters an aspen-bordered meadow which offers a glimpse of Mount Moriah high to the northwest. There are several possible campsites. This would be a good destination for the first day of a two-or three-day trip. The Table and Mount Moriah are within easy reach from this point.

Now climbing a bit more steeply, the trail continues up Hendrys Creek. At about 10,000 feet, the trail enters another, steeper meadow which offers better views. This meadow is the lower end of several large snow avalanche paths which start on Mount Moriah's east face. The trail switchbacks to the east, leaving the meadow, and then climbs up a gentle ridge through an open forest. After crossing a couple of canyons on the northeast slopes of Mount Moriah, it climbs up a final slope to the south rim of The Table.

This 11,000 foot plateau slopes gently to the north and is an open and nearly treeless arctic plain. During the short growing season, alpine flowers such as phlox and blue columbine are common. The south edge of The Table is bordered with twisted, picturesque bristlecone pines. By walking a short distance to the north, you can get a view of most of the surrounding ranges, including Jeff Davis and Wheeler Peak in the South Snake Range. Unlike most high mountain viewpoints, there isn't a view of the surrounding canyons and ridges. The high rim of The Table blocks the nearer view and makes this vantage point seem especially remote.

A sign points back down Hendrys Creek and marks the junction with two cairned trails; the trail to Big Creek on the west, and to Hampton and Horse Creeks on the east. This is the end of the hike.

21 The Table

Although the approach road is long and requires a four-wheel-drive vehicle, this high-elevation trailhead provides the easiest access to The Table and Mount Moriah.

- Distance: 6.2 miles out-and-back
- Time: 4 hours
- Difficulty: Moderate
- Elevation change: 9,900 to 11,000 feet
- Season: Summer and fall
- Permits: None. Hikers should leave word of their hiking plan with a reliable person
- Water: Spring in Big Canyon
- Maps: USGS: Sixmile Canyon, Mount Moriah; USFS: Mount Moriah Wilderness
- Finding the Trailhead: From Baker, drive 5.0 miles northwest on NV 487, then turn left (west) on US 6-50. Continue 14.4 miles, crossing over Sacramento Pass, then turn right on a maintained dirt road. This road starts westward but then turns north along the east side of Spring Valley. Go 12.1 miles, then turn right (east) onto the Fourmile Road, an unmaintained dirt road (Forest Road 469) found just before crossing a cattle guard. Drive east 2.6 miles to the foothills, then bear left. The road crosses a drainage, then climbs to reach a small saddle and a cattle guard after 0.3 miles. To continue beyond this point, you'll need a high-clearance, four-wheel-drive vehicle. The road beyond climbs steeply up a scenic ridge, gaining 2,000 feet in 3.0 miles. At the top of the climb, several minor roads branch left; stay right on the main road. After another 3.2 miles, a minor road turns left; go straight on the main road. In 0.1 miles, you'll pass a small Forest Service cabin on the right in a stand of aspen. The cabin is open to the public and would make a good emergency shelter; please leave it as you found it. Continue 1.9 miles, crossing Deadman Creek, to the signed trailhead at the end of the road. There is a small campsite just north of the trailhead. UTM: Zone 11 740426mE 4353983mN

Key Points

- 0.0 Big Canyon Trailhead (UTM: Zone 11 740426mE 4353983mN)
- 1.1 Spring where trail starts to climb out of Big Canyon (UTM: Zone 11 740969mE 4352327mN)
- 2.1 The Table (UTM: Zone 11 742028mE 4352295mN)
- 3.1 Junction with Hendrys Creek Trail (UTM: Zone 11 743408mE 4351865mN); return the way you came
- 6.2 Big Canyon Trailhead (UTM: Zone 11 740426mE 4353983mN)

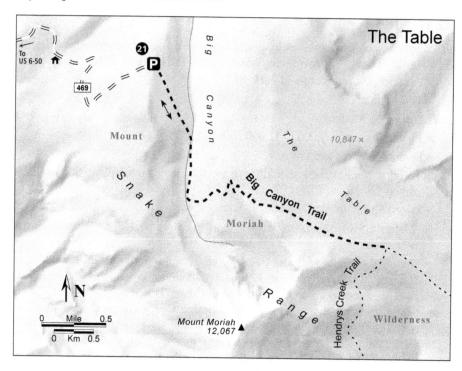

Below Mount Moriah

The Hike

This hike is worth it just for the view from the trailhead. As you start the walk south into Big Canyon, the rugged northwest face of Mount Moriah is framed in the canyon before you. The trail drops gradually into the bottom of Big Canyon, then follows the bed upstream through aspen, fir, and limber pine forest. Big Canyon is normally dry, but there is a small, unnamed spring (not shown on the topographic map) next to the trail just after it turns sharply left and starts to climb the east slopes of the canyon. Climb this steep, switchbacking section for about a mile to reach the southwest rim of The Table. Continue east as the trail skirts the north ridge of Mount Moriah. At first, The Table is graced with a fine stand of gnarled, timberline bristlecone pine, but soon becomes a treeless, arctic plateau. After walking across the plateau for a mile, you'll reach a cairn marking the junction with the Hendrys Creek Trail, which drops south into Hendrys Creek.

With such an easy approach trail, you should have plenty of time to explore The Table. Mount Moriah is an easy, 1,000 foot climb from anywhere along the last mile of this hike. Another great hike is to go out to the north edge of The Table, a walk of about a mile one way. More bristlecone groves skirt the north edge of the plateau, and the view into Deadman Creek and the other tributaries of Smith Creek is excellent. With a car shuttle, you could use the Hendrys Creek Trail to do a two or three day backpack trip traversing the range.

Bristlecone pine on The Table

Winter Touring

Winter is the quiet season in the Snake Range. The upper slopes and mountain summits are covered with snow much of the winter, providing opportunities for backcountry skiing and snowshoeing. Baker Creek Road and Wheeler Peak Scenic Drive are closed to motor vehicles during winter but are open to skiers and snowshoers. Lower Lehman Creek Campground is open in the winter, and Lehman Caves tours are available.

Outdoor recreation is more challenging in winter than other times of the year. Visitors should be be experienced, equipped and prepared for winter weather, which can change rapidly. Backcountry skiers and snowshoers must be aware of possible avalanche hazard on the mountain slopes.

There is no food service in the park during the winter, and the town of Baker has limited services. The nearest town with full services is Ely.

Skiing and Snowshoeing

There are no groomed trails in the park or the Snake Range and skiers and snowshoers must be prepared to handle natural snow conditions. These vary from deep new snow, to powder, to wet or frozen corn snow, or deep slush. Rental equipment may be available in Baker- see the Lodging and Services chapter. For current snow conditions, call 775-234-7331 x 7510.

Fall colors and a dusting of snow on the summits show that winter is on the way

Backcountry Winter Camping

Backcountry campers in the park must follow the Backcountry Guidelines. The Wheeler Peak Day Use Area is closed to camping year round. Backcountry users may camp in the closed Wheeler Peak Campground during the winter at no charge.

Winter Trails and Routes

Remember that winter trails and routes are maintained only by other users. All trails climb to various degrees and there are no level trails. Most winter trailheads are at about 7,000 feet. Routes that leave the main roads are not marked and will require winter navigation skills.

Wheeler Peak Scenic Drive

This route follows the Wheeler Peak Scenic Drive from the winter closure point at Lower Lehman Creek Campground to the end of the road at Wheeler Peak Campground. Some parts of the road are south-facing and may be bare at times. The descent can be icy and fast.

Upper Lehman Creek Campground

The loop road through the campground is a good beginner cross-country ski or snowshoe route. You'll need to ski or snowshoe up the Wheeler Peak Scenic Drive from the winter closure at Lower Lehman Creek Campground.

Lehman Creek Trail

This route uses the Wheeler Peak Scenic Drive to reach the Lehman Creek Trail, a summer hiking trail that follows Lehman Creek from Upper Lehman Creek Campground to Wheeler Peak Campground. The trail can be difficult to follow and the descent can be tricky along the narrow hiking trail.

Alpine Lakes Trail

To reach this trail, you'll first have to ski or snowshoe the Wheeler Peak Scenic Drive from the winter closure point at Lower Lehman Creek Campground to the end of the road at Wheeler Peak Campground. See the Alpine Lakes Trail for a description. This route can be dangerous due to frozen lakes and avalanche danger.

Wheeler Peak

Wheeler Peak in winter is a serious winter mountaineering trip. It requires skiing or snowshoeing the Wheeler Peak Scenic Drive from the winter closure point at Lower Lehman Creek Campground to the Summit Trailhead, and then ascending the Wheeler Peak Trail to the summit. Note that camping is not allowed any time of year in the Wheeler Peak Day Use Area, but free winter camping is available at the end of the road in Wheeler Peak Campground. Only those experienced and equipped for winter mountaineering should attempt this route. Use caution for potentially high avalanche danger.

Caving

Wild Caves

There are more than 40 wild caves in the park- of these, one is currently open to the caving public and the rest are closed due to White-Nose Syndrome. Caves that are open to the public are closed certain times of the year to protect native bat populations.

White-Nose Syndrome

White-Nose Syndrome (WNS) is a fungal disease that has killed more than a million bats in North America since it was detected in 2006. This epidemic started in upstate New York and has since spread west to Oklahoma. WNS causes bats to behave in unusual ways and in some cases has killed over 90 percent of the bats in a cave. Bats make up more than 20 percent of the mammal species on Earth and consume enough insects to save the U.S. agricultural industry over 3 billion dollars a year in pest-control.

Little Muddy Cave is currently the only wild cave in the park open to cavers. It is open from October 1 to April 1.

Cave Permits

The park will issue a cave permit to those who can demonstrate their experience with horizontal and vertical caving techniques, expertise with the required equipment, and cave conservation ethics. Cavers must certify that their equipment is clean and disinfected.The permit must be in your possession while caving. Permits must be applied for at least one week before the caving trip. Only one permit per week will be issued for each cave. Groups entering a wild cave must have a minimum of three members, and a maximum of six members. A separate cave permit is required for each cave.

Cave permit terms and regulations, and cave permit application forms, are available at home.nps.gov/grba/planyourvisit/caving.htm. For more information contact Resource Management staff at 775-234-7331 x 7561. Mail permit applications to:

Resource Management

Great Basin National Park

100 Great Basin National Park

Baker, NV 89311

Lehman Caves are just one of many caves in the park

Technical Climbing

Technical rock climbing is allowed in the park but is not a popular activity. This is due to the remoteness of the area and the looseness of the rock. All routes in the Wheeler Peak area are dangerous with deadly rock fall all year. Check with either of the visitor centers for more information.

Park Climbing Regulations

Climbers should remember that the primary purpose of Great Basin National Park is to preserve its outstanding resources and significant geological and scenic values. All biological, cultural, and mineral resources are protected in their natural state. To help accomplish this task, the park asks that climbers follow these regulations:

- Chiseling, chipping, gluing, or breaking away rock, or otherwise physically altering the rock, is prohibited. This includes placing bolts or other fixed protection. Clean aid, top-roping, or traditional lead climbing are permitted.

- The use of motorized drills, hand drills or other portable motorized equipment is not allowed.

- Painting or otherwise marking the rock including names of climbs or ratings is prohibited.

- Climbing within 100 yards of an archaeological site, including pictographs and petroglyphs, is not permitted.

- Damaging plant life, including lichens and moss, is prohibited.

There are no specific climbing regulations on the Humboldt-Toiyabe National Forest. In the Mount Moriah Wilderness, use of mechanized equipment, including power drills, is prohibited.

Climbing Registration

Registering for technical climbs in the park is voluntary, but climbers are strongly encouraged to register at one of the visitor centers. Registration provides vital information for rescue teams.

If using chalk, pick a color that blends in with the dominant gray limestone in the park. Use muted color webbing or rope for rappel anchors.

In a climbing emergency, contact any ranger, campground host, or visitor center, or call 911. A pay phone is located at Lehman Cave Visitor Center. All climbers should be prepared for climbing in remote areas and be capable of self-rescue. Mountain rescue resources are limited and rescue teams may be hours away.

Resources

Land Management Agencies

Great Basin National Park

100 Great Basin National Park
Baker, NV 89311
775-234-7331
www.nps.gov/grba

Humboldt-Toiyabe National Forest

825 Avenue E
Ely, NV 89301
775-289-3031
www.fs.fed.us/r4/htnf/

Bureau of Land Management

702 N Industrial Way
Ely, NV 89301
775-289-1800
www.blm.gov/office/ely-district-office

Private Organizations

Western National Parks Association

12880 North Vistoso Village Drive
Tucson, AZ 85755
520-622-1999
info@wnpa.org
www.wnpa.org

Great Basin Heritage Area

P.O. Box 78
Baker, Nevada 89311
775-234-7171
info@greatbasinheritage.org
www.greatbasinheritage.org

Maps

USGS Topographic Maps

www.usgs.gov/pubprod/maps.html

Digital Maps

CalTopo.com
GaiaGPS.com

Books

Castaldo, Nancy F., Deserts: An Activity Guide for Ages 6-9, Chicago Review Press, 2004.

Fox, William L., The Void, The Grid & The Sign: Traversing The Great Basin, University of Nevada Press, 2005.

Larmbert, Darwin, Great Basin Drama: The Story of a National Park, Roberts Rinehart Publishers, 1991.

Nicklas, Michael L.; Van Camp, Mary L. ; Dooven, K.C. Den; Great Basin: The Story Behind the Scenery, KC Publications, 1996.

Waring, Gwendolyn L., A Natural History of the Intermountain West: Its Ecological and Evolutionary Story, University of Utah Press, 2011.

Also by the Author

Books

Exploring With GPS: A Practical Field Guide for Satellite Navigation

Exploring Grand Canyon: From Lees Ferry to the Grand Wash Cliffs

Publish! How To Publish Your Book as an E-Book on the Amazon Kindle and in Print with CreateSpace

Websites

BruceGrubbs.com

BrightAngelPress.com

CanyonLightPhotography.com

ExploringGreatBasin.net

ExploringGrandCanyon.info

ExploringGps.com

Before You Go

Please consider leaving a review for this book on Amazon at amzn.to/23Vzt7P. I would greatly appreciate it.

And, if you want to be the first to know about my new books, as well as revisions, consider signing up for my mailing list at eepurl.com/bPW7dD. This list will only be used for that purpose- I will NEVER spam you or share the list with anyone. You can unsubscribe at any time.

About the Author

The author has a serious problem- he doesn't know what he wants to do when he grows up. Meanwhile, he's done such things as wildland fire fighting, running a mountain shop, flying airplanes, shooting photos, and writing books. He's a backcountry skier, climber, figure skater, mountain biker, amateur radio operator, river runner, and sea kayaker- but the thing that really floats his boat is hiking and backpacking. No matter what else he tries, the author always comes back to hiking-especially long, rough, cross-country trips in places like the Grand Canyon. Some people never learn. But what little he has learned, he's willing to share with you- via his books, of course, but also via his websites, blogs, and whatever works.

The author on Wheeler Peak

Index

airlines 21
Alpine Lakes 103
Baker 17
Baker Creek 114
Baker Lake 114
bookstores 25
bristlecone pines 109
bus 21
campfires 81
campgrounds, commercial 48
campsites, primitive 47
Can Young Canyon 121
climate 10
cross-country skiing 145
driving to the park 21
Egan, Howard R. 14
elevations 10
emigrants 14
entrance fees 25
Fremont, John Charles 14
government surveys 14
Great Basin National Park 17
Hendrys Creek 138
hikes, recommended 84
hiking permits 77
hiking regulations 77
Humboldt River 14
Humboldt-Toiyabe National Forest 17
Johnson Lake 114, 123
Junior Ranger programs 51
Lehman Caves National Monument 17
Lehman Creek 92
Lehman, Absalom S. 15
Lexington Arch 134
life zones 29
loggers 15
miners 15
Mount Moriah 140, 143
Mount Moriah Wilderness 18, 135
Muir, John 15
Osceola Ditch 88
Osceola tunnel 85
Pole Canyon 119

Pony Express 14
precipitation 11
prehistory 12
railroad 14
rental cars 21
RV dump stations 43
settlement 15
showers 43
Simpson, Captain James H. 14
Smith Creek 134
Snake Creek 124, 128
Snake Valley 17
snowshoeing 145
South Fork Big Wash 131
Spanish 13
Spring Valley 17
Stella Lake 104
Strawberry Creek 87
Teresa Lake 104
The Table 140, 143
thunderstorms 11
Timber Creek 115, 117
traders 13
trappers 13
visitor centers 25
water 79
weather 10, 81
WebRanger 51
Wheeler Icefield 109
Wheeler Peak 99
Wheeler, George M. 14

CPSIA information can be obtained
at www.ICGtesting.com
Printed in the USA
FSHW022012091020
74686FS